Cocorico Early Frenc
(5-11 years)

A learning and teaching guide
full of easy instructions
and fun activities

Cocorico!
Book 1

By Zara Mercer and Margaret McKee

About the Book

This book is a useful guide for **classroom teachers** and **parents** who need **inspiration and new ideas, to teach children from 5 to 10 years old.**
It is the first of three books and has been conceived with both the **Novice** and **Specialist French Teacher** in mind. The scheme of work in this book conforms to the English National Curriculum guidelines of:-

The book is divided into **8 chapters.**

The step-by-step instructions are simple to follow. Every lesson is clearly set out with a **"vocabulaire"** section at the beginning, followed by clear **"teaching ideas"**, a list of **materials** needed for the lesson, and a choice of different **"activités"** and games both written and oral. There are resource sheets and worksheets to accompany the lesson plans.

Every lesson should begin with **"Greetings and Revision"**. This gives the children an opportunity to get straight into the French spirit with the teacher and classmates as well as going over previously covered lessons. This is when the children can participate in a quick and lively activities. Oral **'question-and-answer'** and other appropriate activities are suggested in the section at the beginning of the lesson.

"Teaching Ideas" is the principle part of the lesson. It facilitates the application of the objectives. However, sometimes a discussion in which the children share their ideas or experiences relating to the topic is a useful introduction to the subject.

Every lesson involves **vocabulary repetition**. This can be made more interesting, not only by using the various **resources** mentioned above, but also by engaging the children in other **activities** such as songs, worksheets, role-plays or games as suggested in each topic. Younger children especially enjoy handling toys and objects and they participate more readily as a result.

Contents

Topic	Leçon	Title	Page
Toi et Moi	1	Je m'appelle	1
	2	Ça va?	4
	3	Quel âge as-tu?	7
	4	Où habites-tu?	9
Les couleurs	1	L'arc-en-ciel	10
Ma Famille	1	Les Membres de ma Famille	15
	2	La Famille	17
	3	La Grande Famille	20
Mon Anniversaire	1	Les Nombres	28
	2	Les Jours de la Semaine	33
	3	Les Mois	37
Dans ma Classe	1	La Classe	43
	2	Dans ma trousse il y a …	46
	3	Dans mon école	50
Au Café	1	Que désires-tu?	52
	2	Je voudrais	55
En France	1	La Culture	62
	2	La Fête de fin d'année	65
Les Fêtes	1	Les Jours de Vacances	68
	2	La fête nationale	70
	3	Noël	71

TOI ET MOI
Leçon 1
"Je m'appelle"

Vocabulaire

Comment t'appelles-tu?
What is your name?
Je m'appelle ...
My name is ...

Bonjour *Hello*	**Au revoir** *Good-bye*
Salut! *Hi!*	**Moi** *Me*
Les enfants *The children*	**Madame** *Mrs.*
Et toi? *And you?*	**Monsieur** *Mr.*

Teaching Ideas

Say **"Bonjour les enfants. Je m'appelle Madame/Monsieur ..."** Go around the class greeting each child with
"Bonjour! Comment t'appelles-tu?"

Encourage each child to reply with a greeting and their name eg

"Bonjour! Je m'appelle Claire"

Tell the children that they can greet their friends by saying **"Salut!"** which is French for "Hi!".

However, explain that they should always greet you and other adults with "Bonjour".

"Je m'appelle..."
Encourage the children to say **"Je m'appelle ..."**, perhaps even **"Salut! Je m'appelle"**. The children can stand in a circle or sit in a line and practise the dialogue below:

    Child 1 turns to child 2 and says **"Salut! Je m'appelle..."**
    Child 2 then says, **"Salut! Je m'appelle ..."** to child 3
    Child 3 in turn repeats this to child 4 and so it continues down the line

"Comment t'appelles-tu?"
Now the children ask the question **"Comment t'appelles-tu?"** See the dialogue below. Instead of always repeating **"Comment t'appelles-tu?"**, after they have given their name they can find out the other person's name by simply saying **"et toi?"** - **get the children to shake hands.**

Divide the class into small groups to practise the following dialogue:

Child 1:	"Comment t'appelles-tu?"
Child 2:	"Je m'appelle ... et toi?
Child 1:	"Je m'appelle ..."
Child 2:	"Comment t'appelles-tu?"
Child 3:	"Je m'appelle ... et toi?"

"Au revoir"
Tell the children that at the end of every lesson they cannot leave the class without saying:
"Au revoir" in answer to your **"Au revoir les enfants"**.

"Je m'appelle"

"Je m'appelle Cocorico"

Children form a circle. One child stands in the centre and wears a blindfold. He/she spins around while counting to 5 in French and then walks forward and touches a child in the circle and asks **"Comment t'appelles-tu?"**. The child in the circle must then respond by saying "Je m'appelle **Cocorico**". The blindfolded child must guess the real name of "Cocorico". When Cocorico's real name is guessed, they swap places, and the game continues.

"Cercle de noms"

Children form a circle. The teacher stands in the centre (later a child can stand there) and **throws a ball** or bean bag **to a child in the circle** while asking **"Comment t'appelles-tu?"** the child catches the ball or bean bag and answers **"Je m'appelle…."** and then throws the ball back to the teacher. The teacher continues throwing the ball around the circle until each child has had a turn at catching the ball and saying their name.

"C'est Moi"

Choose a friend to draw your picture in the square below and then ask them to autograph it.

Voici mon portrait par ....

TOI ET MOI
Leçon 2
"Ça va?"

Vocabulaire

Ça va?
How are you?

Ça va bien
I'm well

Ça va mal
I'm not well

...et toi?
...and you?

Ça va bien merci
Very well thank you

Comme-ci comme-ça
So-so

GREETINGS, REVISION ROLE PLAY

Greet the children with **"Bonjour les enfants"**. Remind them to greet the teacher with **"Bonjour Madame/Monsieur"** and their friends with **Salut!**.

Ask the children if they can remember what **"Comment t'appelles-tu?"** means. Now ask them to give you the correct answer to that question:
   "Je m'appelle..."
Always praise the correct answer with **"Bien / très bien / bravo!"**.

Choose two children, one will be named **"moi"** and the other **"toi"**. Remind them what these words mean.

"Moi" begins by saying:-
   "Moi, je m'appelle ... et toi, comment t'appelles-tu?" To this "toi" replies:-
   "Je m'appelle ..."
A toy animal/puppet/doll can be introduced to say the words. The children should learn to ask the correct question.

Teaching Ideas

Explain to the children that **in France it is usual to kiss** a friend they meet on both cheeks, asking **"Ça va?"**, to which the reply is **"Ça va bien"**, **"Comme-ci comme-ça"** or **"Ça va mal"**. Repeat this a couple of times and encourage the children to follow suit.
A typical conversation between two children could be:

   "Salut Jean, ça va?"
   "Salut Robert, oui ça va bien, et toi ?"

However, if they are not feeling well they could say **"ça va mal"**
A useful prompt to help the children remember how to say **"ça va bien"** is to make a **thumbs-up** sign and **smile broadly**. Also prompt the children to say **"ça va mal"** with a **thumbs down** sign and **a sad face**. **"Comme ci comme ça"** is indicated by holding both hands out in front, palms down and tipping them from side to side. Children who are shy find it easier initially to use these signs when asked how they are. (See page 6)

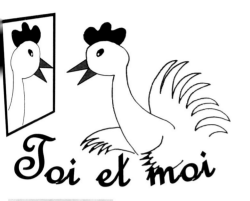

"Ça va?"

 "Comment ça va?"

> **Materials:** Copies of "Comment ça va" flashcards page 6, 3 cards per person.

Shuffle and distribute the cards. Child 1 starts the game by asking Child 2 "Comment ça va?". Child 2 chooses a card from his or her hand and gives the answer to match it. He / She shows the card and puts it down. He / She then asks child 3 the question "Comment ça va?". The game continues this way until all the cards have been used.

 "Pairs"

> **Materials:** Copy and cut out 2 to 4 copies of "Comment ça va" Flashcards page 6.

Play a game of pairs with the flashcards. Place the cards face down on the table. The children in turn have to turn over two cards and name them. If both cards match, they keep the pair and the game continues. The winner is the one with the most pairs.

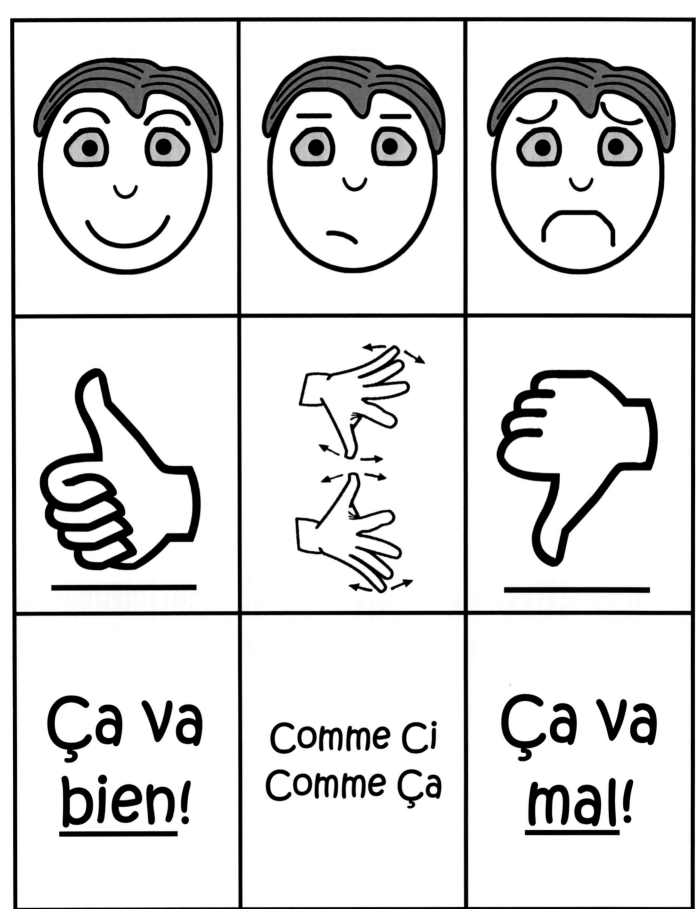

TOI ET MOI
Leçon 3
"Quel âge as-tu?"

Vocabulaire

Ecoute bien
Listen carefully

Quel âge as-tu?
How old are you?

J'ai ... ans	Quatre	Neuf
I am ...	4	9
years old	Cinq	Dix
Un	5	10
1	Six	Onze
Deux	6	11
2	Sept	Douze
Trois	7	12
3	Huit	
	8	

GREETINGS, REVISION

"Bonjour les enfants. Ça va ?"
"Bonjour madame/monsieur. Oui ça va bien/ça va mal."
Children greet each other with **"Salut"**. For a quick conversation warm-up go around the class asking each child a question such as:

"Comment t'appelles-tu?"
(And to the next:) "Et toi?"
or
"Ça va bien?"
or
"Ça va mal?"

The children must give the correct reply.

J'ai sept ans!

Teaching Ideas

Encourage the children to clap and count with you as you count from 1 – 6 in French. Repeat this two or three times. Then repeat this exercise while counting to 12 with the children. Explain to the class that you are going to **clap your hands** a certain number of times and they need to **listen** carefully, point to your ears and say **"Ecoutez bien"**. Clap 6 times and ask the children to **guess the number of claps** using the numbers they have just learnt. The child who guesses the correct number gets a turn to clap (1 – 12) and can then ask another child to guess the number of claps.

Go around the class asking several children in turn **"Quel âge as-tu?"**. Tell them that the answer to that is **"J'ai ... ans (six/sept/huit/neuf/dix/onze etc)"**
Ask each child in turn the same question prompting them with the correct numbers.

Alternatively, each child can take a partner and practice a short role-play using the question and answer phrases **"Quel âge as-tu? and J'ai ... ans"**

Number songs are a useful aid to learning the numbers. For example, the numbers from 1-10 can be sung to the tune of **'Frère Jacques'** (page 29).

Cocorico Books © Zara Mercer & Margaret Mckee 2009

Sept

"QUEL ÂGE AS-TU?"

"Jeu de 1 à 12"

Materials: Flashcards numbered from 1 to 12 (one per child) page 30.

Give each child a flashcard: Call out a number from 1 to 12 (at random). The players with that card hold it up and say the number out loud.
To make this game more interesting, the teacher can call the numbers out in English and the children respond in French or vice versa.

"Salade de Fruits"

Arrange chairs for each child except one **in a circle**. Each child sits down except the last who **stands in the centre**. The children are given a number 1 to 12 (fewer numbers can be used for a smaller group). At least two children should share a number. When their number is called they cross the circle and swap seats with those with the same number. The child **standing in the centre** of the circle must attempt to 'steal' a vacated chair and if successful he/she sits in the circle leaving a new child in the centre. When the teacher calls out **"Salade!"**, all the children must swap places.

N.B. the child in the centre has 3 turns then he/she must be replaced.

"Salade" (a variation of the above)

The children sit on chairs arranged in a **large circle**. The teacher chooses three or four numbers, for example **"deux, trois, quatre / huit, neuf, dix"**. Each child is given one of the three numbers to **remember** - several children will of course have the same number. The teacher **calls out a number** and all the children with that number get up and **change places** with each other. A second number is called and all those with that number **swap** places, this is repeated until each child has changed his/her seat. Finally the teacher says **"salade de fruits"** and all the children cross the circle to a different chair. However while everyone is moving the teacher goes into the circle and sits down on one of the chairs. This means that one child will not have a chair and will be **'out'**. A chair is taken away and the game continues until only **2 children are left.** They are the winners

N.B. as the game progresses and the numbers disappear, a child may find he / she no longer has anyone to swap with. When this happens all they need to do when their number is called, is to get up and go into the centre of the circle and then back to their chair.

Cocorico Books © Zara Mercer & Margaret Mckee 2009

Vocabulaire

Où habites-tu?
Where do you live?

J'habite à... (ville)
I live in... (town)

Elle/Il habite à...
She/he lives in...

...et toi?
...and you?

En Angleterre
In England

En Espagne
In Spain

En Allemagne
In Germany

En Italie
In Italy

GREETINGS, REVISION ROLE PLAY

Children can revise previous lessons with the teacher by repeating and practising the dialogue below:-

Child 1 - Salut / Bonjour. Je m'appelle ... et toi?
Child 2 - Je m'appelle ...
Child 1 - Quel âge as-tu?
Child 2 - J'ai ... ans, et toi?
Child 1 - Moi, j'ai ... ans. J'habite à ... et toi, où habites-tu?
Child 2 - J'habite à...

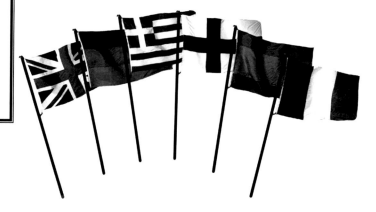

Teaching Ideas

La ville (The town)

Explain to the children that they are going to find out where everyone in the class lives. Start this off by asking the question **"Où habites-tu?"**, the answer from the children should be **"J'habite à ... "**, (name of their town).
N.B do not translate the names of towns into French; keep the English name.
However London is translated into Londres. The children can now practise a dialogue in pairs (or groups of 4):

    Child 1 - "Où habites-tu?"
    Child 2 - "J'habite à ... et toi?"

To take this a step further:-

Le pays (The country)

When asked **"Où habites-tu?"** the answer can be **"J'habite à Exeter en Angleterre"** (en France / en Allemagne / en Italie etc.)

Ma Carte d'identité

NATIONALITÉ ....

COMMENT T'APPELLES-TU? *(Nom)* ....

OÙ HABITES-TU? *(Adresse)* ....

QUEL ÂGE AS-TU? ....

EN QUELLE DATE ES-TU NÉ(E)? *(Date de naissance)* ....

OÙ ES-TU NÉ(E)? *(Lieu de naissance)* ....

LOISIR PRÉFÉRÉ ....

SPORT PRÉFÉRÉ ....

COULEUR PRÉFÉRÉE ....

Signature

LES COULEURS
Leçon 1
"L'arc-en-ciel"

GREETINGS, REVISION

After the usual greetings and counting go over the dialogue:-

"Où habites-tu?"
"J'habite à ..."

Also practice "**quel âge as-tu?**" and "**ça va?**" using some of the children's favourite games from previous lessons.

Vocabulaire

Touche quelque chose de rouge
Touch something red
Et voici les couleurs
And here are the colours
C'est quelle couleur?
What colour is it?

Orange	**Vert**	**Violet**
Orange	*Green*	*Purple*
Rouge	**Marron**	**Gris**
Red	*Brown*	*Grey*
Bleu	**Noir**	**Foncé**
Blue	*Black*	*Dark*
Jaune	**Blanc**	**Clair**
Yellow	*White*	*Light*

Teaching Ideas

Materials: Large squares of card in a variety of colours to use as flash cards

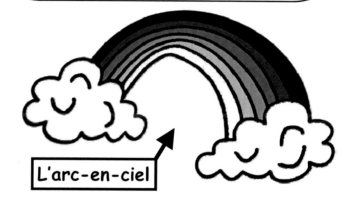

L'arc-en-ciel

Choose 8 children to stand at the front of the class in a row and give them each a **coloured flashcard** (alternatively the children hold up a coloured pencil). Sing the song **"Les couleurs"**, encourage the children to **hold up** their cards (or pencils) every time their colour is mentioned in the song.

When the children have learnt the song and the colours quite well, ask them to arrange themselves in a row **according to the sequence of the colours in the song.**

Tell the children to **touch** a **certain colour** somewhere in the room. **"Touchez quelque chose de rouge"** e.g. all the children run to find that colour. Continue like this until most of the colours learnt have been found somewhere in the classroom.

Chantez!
Les couleurs
(to the tune of Three Blind Mice)

Orange, rouge, bleu,
Orange, rouge, bleu,
Jaune, vert, marron,
Jaune, vert, marron,
Et voilà toutes les couleurs,
Et voilà toutes les couleurs,
Noir et blanc.

Colours not mentioned in the song can still be taught using flashcards or the exercise above. Make sure the children repeat the colours eg Say **"C'est gris!"**, a few times then ask them **"C'est quelle couleur?"**, for each colour.

"L'ARC-EN-CIEL"

Les couleurs

"Le sac de couleurs"

> Materials: Large bag (*Le sac de couleurs*) filled with lots (about 40 or 50) of different coloured squares (card or felt)

"Quelle couleur?"

Pass "**le sac**" around the class, each child **takes out a square** and **says the colour in French**. If they are correct, they keep the square. This can also be played as a team game. The child or team with the most squares wins.

"Devine la couleur"

The teacher/pupil holds out **le sac de couleurs** and says **"Devinez la couleur"**. Every child picks a colour. The teacher then **pulls out a square.**
One point is awarded to each child that has **guessed correctly**. After 5 rounds the child with the most points wins. This game is easily repeated.

"Stop!"

Spread lots of different coloured squares on a flat surface. The first team **looks away while the another team selects a square**. It is left untouched. The first team then starts to **pick** up the squares one by one **saying the colour out loud**. They keep picking up squares until they touch the selected square at which point the other team calls out **"stop!"**. The squares collected are counted up. The aim is to collect as many squares as possible by avoiding the selected square.
N.B. This game can also be played by aiming to collect the least amount of squares possible before touching the chosen square. The winner would being the team with the fewest cards collected.

"Les couleurs en musique"

> Materials: Large coloured squares
> CD Player

Scatter the **large coloured squares** on the floor. Play some French **music**.
The teacher **secretly chooses a colour, writes it down** and then **stops the music**. The children **run** to a **square** of their choice. The teacher then **reveals the colour** and **anyone standing next to that colour is out**. The game continues until a winner is found (i.e. the last child still in the game) The children who are out can then help the teacher continue with the game.
N.B. A faster alternative is to send out the children who are not standing by the chosen colour.

 Cocorico Books © Zara Mercer & Margaret Mckee 2009   **Douze**

Mots Mêlés

Les Couleurs

- 13 -

E	L	V	N	B	F	V	T	L	O	N	C	R	V	X
Q	V	K	E	Q	T	A	O	Q	R	O	X	B	C	L
P	V	E	W	R	L	Q	O	E	A	I	P	D	H	J
Y	I	I	B	O	T	K	L	A	N	R	D	T	D	C
K	O	Y	I	E	S	L	Q	M	G	U	T	S	B	Y
R	L	D	O	M	L	B	Z	J	E	X	Q	A	D	K
O	E	H	R	O	S	E	S	E	D	X	S	K	I	M
Q	T	L	D	A	X	P	U	B	L	A	N	C	Z	J
I	F	Z	R	O	U	G	E	A	W	S	W	F	R	A
Y	Q	V	L	D	V	A	O	X	N	P	Q	L	V	U
V	G	C	O	U	H	H	B	U	Q	L	M	A	Z	N
M	A	R	R	O	N	K	Q	L	D	G	R	A	E	E
A	P	K	I	W	P	G	Q	J	E	R	R	B	S	E
Y	C	O	U	L	E	U	R	S	F	U	U	I	Q	Q
Q	L	U	A	E	C	F	U	Z	L	E	V	E	S	N

blanc   noir   rouge
gris   orange   vert
jaune   rose   violet
marron   bleu   couleurs

Cocorico Books © Zara Mercer & Margaret Mckee 2009

Coloriez

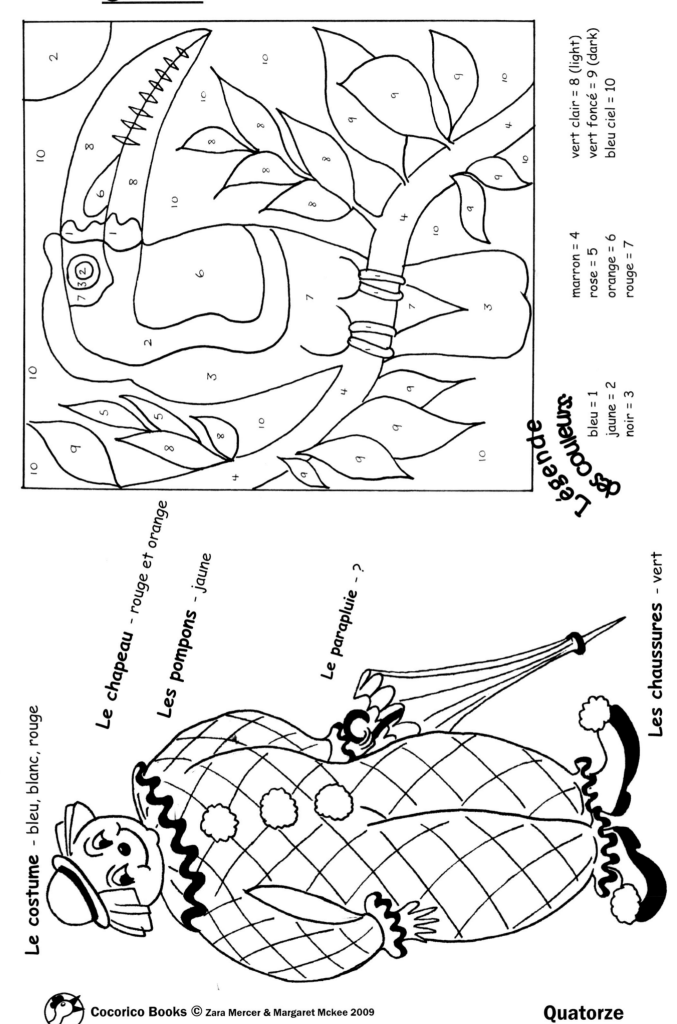

vert clair = 8 (light)
vert foncé = 9 (dark)
bleu ciel = 10

marron = 4
rose = 5
orange = 6
rouge = 7

bleu = 1
jaune = 2
noir = 3

Légende & couleurs

Le costume - bleu, blanc, rouge
Le chapeau - rouge et orange
Les pompons - jaune
Le parapluie - ?
Les chaussures - vert

Quatorze

MA FAMILLE
Leçon 1
"Les membres de ma famille"

Vocabulaire

Il y a combien de personnes dans ta famille?
How many are there in your family?

Dans ma famille il y a ... personnes
There are ... people in my family

Ma famille — *My family*
Mon père — *My father*
Ma mère — *My mother*
Mon frère — *My brother*
Ma soeur — *My sister*
Voici — *Here is*
Je suis — *I am*

GREETINGS, REVISION ROLE PLAY

Remind the children to greet you with **"Bonjour!"** and their friends with **"Salut!"**. Ask them **"Ça va?"** Choose a child to come forward and count how many people are in the class.

Using a quick question-and-answer exercise go around the class asking "Quel âge as-tu? / Comment t'appelles-tu?/ Où habites-tu?"

The teacher could throw a ball to different children when asking the questions.

Tell the children to bring photos or pictures of their families

Teaching Ideas

Materials: Copy of "La Famille Durand" (page 18)
Or family pictures from magazines

Tell the children that today you are going to talk about **the family "La famille"**.
Show the class the **picture of the Durand family**, (or pictures from magazines).
Point to each person in turn and say the words e.g. **"Voici la mère / le père"** etc. Get the children to repeat after you.
Ask the children to **count** the **number of people in the family**.
Then say **"Dans la famille il y a 6 personnes"**

The children now need to say how many people they have in **their** family. Start asking each child **"Il y a combien de personnes dans ta famille?"**. Help them with the answer **"Dans ma famille il y a ... personnes"**. They list the people by saying **"Il y a ma mère / mon père / ma soeur / mon frère"**. The family picture (or the children's pictures) can be shown again to demonstrate this.

 Cocorico Books © Zara Mercer & Margaret Mckee 2009   Quinze

"Les membres de ma famille"

~ "Voici la famille" ~

Materials: Paper (1 sheet per child), pencils and colours

Draw a quick **sketch on the board of a family of four** (see below)
Label each character e.g. la mère / le père / la soeur / le frère.
Now **ask the children to draw the four members of a family** on the paper and then to label them. (Encourage the children to make their family distinctive)

Le père · · · · · La mère · · · · · Le frère · · · · · La soeur

~ "Jeu de mémoire" ~

Materials: Drawings of the four members of a family (from the activity above)

Using the children's drawings **cut out each family member**.
Divide the class into groups of four. Each child chooses one of their own drawings to complete a family and holds it up saying for example: **"Voici le père"**.
The second player repeats this and adds the name of their chosen family member eg. **"Voici le père *et la mère*"** the game continues like this until everyone in the group has said the sentence and added one family member.
The children can repeat the activity using another one of their drawings.

Cocorico Books © Zara Mercer & Margaret Mckee 2009   **Seize**

MA FAMILLE
Leçon 2
"La famille"

Vocabulaire

Avez-vous des grands-parents?
Do you have grandparents?

Avez-vous une tante et un oncle?
Do you have an aunt and an uncle?

Les grands-parents
Grandparents

Ma grand-mère
My grandmother

Mon grand-père
My grandfather

Ma tante
My aunt

Mon oncle
My uncle

Ma cousine
My cousin

Qui est-ce?
Who is it?

C'est ...
It is ...

GREETINGS, REVISION ROLE PLAY

- "Bonjour"
- "Ça va?"
- "Quel âge as-tu?"
- "Combien de personnes il y a dans ta famille?"

Hold up a flashcard of "La famille Durand" page 18 ask a child **"Où est la mère/où est le père?" "Comment s'appelle la mère/le père?"** He/she points to the people on the flashcard and answers the question.

Using **photos** of their **own family**, the children introduce each member to the class by saying:-

"Voici ma mère (elle s'appelle.....), voici mon père (il s'appelle ...)"

Materials: A copy of "La Famille de Luc" page 19

Teaching Ideas

Using "La Famille de Luc", **introduce the extended family**.
Point to the various relations and encourage the children to **repeat after you**:

"voici les grands-parents – la grand-mère et le grand-père."

Repeat this with the other relatives. Ask the children **"Qui est-ce?"**, to which they reply **"C'est la cousine / la tante"** etc

Cocorico Books © Zara Mercer & Margaret Mckee 2009

La famille de Luc

Cut out the pictures and enlarge for use as flashcards

MA FAMILLE
Leçon 3
"La grande famille"

Vocabulaire

Voici la grand-mère de...
Here is the grandmother of...
Voici le grand-père de...
Here is the grandfather of ...
Voici l'oncle de ...
Here is the uncle of ...
Voici la cousine de ...
Here is the cousin of ...
Voici le fils de ...
Here is the son of ...
Voici la fille de ...
Here is the daughter of ...
Qui est la grand-mère de ... ?
Who is the grand mother of ... ?
Qui est le père de ... ?
Who is the father of ... ?

GREETINGS, REVISION

As everyone greets each other **revise La famille** using the picture **"La Famille Durand" page 18**

Point to a person and ask
"qui est-ce?" children should reply
"C'est..." (la mère/le père etc)
See "Jeu de mémoire" page 16 and role-play a family. Each member introduces him/herself eg. **"Je suis la mère"**, **"Je suis le père"** etc.

Ma grande famille!

Teaching Ideas

Materials: "La famille de Luc" flashcards page 19

Using the pictures show the **relationship between the different members of the family**. Holding up the flashcards ask the children questions such as

"Qui est Marie?"
"Comment s'appelle la mère de Josiane?"
"La grand-mère de Luc est........"
"Qui est Sylvie?"
"Comment s'appelle le grand-père de Luke?"
"Comment s'appelle le bébé?"
"Paul est le père ou le grand-père de Luke?"

Cocorico Books © Zara Mercer & Margaret Mckee 2009

"La grande famille"

Dessine les membres de ta famille ou colle leurs photos ici:

Cocorico Books © Zara Mercer & Margaret Mckee 2009

Vingt et un

"LA GRANDE FAMILLE"

 "Je suis ... "

> Materials: Set of flashcards page 26-27 "Jeu des 3 familles"

Distribute all the **flashcards**. Each child **takes his or her place** in the **correct row** according to his or her **position in the family** (on their card), thus forming three separate **family trees** according to which family they are in (**Ballon / Parapluie / Chapeau**) :-

"Grandparents" line up in a row.
"Parents" line up in the row in front of the grandparents.
The "Children" line up in front of the parents.

Then each child **introduces** his / her **character** (acting the part) eg:

"Je suis la grand-mère de la famille Chapeau"
"Je suis le père de la famille Ballon"
"Je suis la fille de la famille Parapluie"

N.B. The children use their props when introducing their character

"Loto des 3 familles"

> Materials: Enlarge and copy two sets of "Loto des 3 familles" page 25

Cut one copy of the loto page into 6 loto boards, then cut the **other copy into 36 separate cards.** Distribute the boards one per child / group depending on numbers. **Shuffle the 36 cards.** Pick out one card at a time and **call out each one naming the family member and the family that they belong to** for instance "**La mère parapluie**", "**Le père chapeau**" and so on. The first child to **call out "Ici!"**, who has the **matching card on their loto board takes it.** He or she **places it face down** on the **corresponding image** on **their board**. The first player to cover all 6 images on their board wins.

N.B. Members of the family on "Loto des 3 familles" page 25, are numbered according to their rank. 1 is "Le Père", 2 is "La mère" etc. Every member of "La famille Chapeau", is wearing a hat, "Famille Ballon", have a ball and "Famille Parapluie", an umbrella.

 Cocorico Books © Zara Mercer & Margaret Mckee 2009

Vingt-deux

L'arbre généalogique

1) Josiane est la .... de Claire.
2) Marie est la .... de Philippe.
3) Sylvie est la .... de Louise.
4) Marc est l' .... de Luc.
5) Louise est la .... de Luc.
6) Charles est le .... de Philippe.
7) Marie et Paul sont les .... de Marc.
8) Milou est le .... de Luc.

Mère, Père, Frère, Sœur, Oncle, Tante, Parents, Grand-mère, Grand-père, Cousin, Cousine.

Mots Mêlés

La Famille

F	Q	V	Q	D	R	G	F	J	A	V	L	B	O	T
G	A	I	C	U	R	R	I	O	R	Z	H	C	G	Z
P	U	M	E	V	B	P	L	J	K	D	Q	T	C	R
J	Q	O	I	I	O	G	S	O	B	F	A	E	X	C
M	S	D	S	L	E	F	T	V	W	Y	J	P	Z	M
P	E	R	E	A	L	R	K	A	K	D	Y	H	C	R
P	R	D	G	L	G	E	K	S	X	B	Q	B	C	B
H	O	Q	X	R	R	R	O	C	F	C	N	T	V	T
G	O	U	M	A	A	E	S	Z	F	R	B	Q	C	E
U	U	N	S	Y	N	N	W	Y	I	Z	E	D	R	E
G	C	E	C	E	D	S	D	K	L	Q	E	T	G	Q
M	P	Y	V	L	M	U	B	P	L	R	E	E	E	G
G	E	R	N	Y	E	K	Z	J	E	C	U	Z	H	Y
W	M	R	U	S	R	H	P	B	N	R	D	J	N	Q
Q	Z	O	E	X	E	E	T	A	N	T	E	X	M	T

(la) grand-mère   (la) tante   (le) fils
(le) grand-père   (l')oncle   (le) frère
(la) soeur   (la) fille

Loto des 3 familles

Photocopy (and enlarge) the boards above. Cut each board out and play Loto des 3 familles as instructed on page 22.

Jeu des Trois Familles

How to play: Photocopy, cut out and distribute cards to each group of three children (colour-in, time permitting) Shuffle and distribute the cards equally. The aim of the game is to collect as many complete families as possible. When it is their turn, children ask (in French) for a card missing from their hand to help complete a family they want from another child. The child asked must hand over the card if he/she has it. If the child asked doesn't have the card, it is the next child's turn to play.

Cocorico Books © Zara Mercer & Margaret Mckee 2009

Vingt-sept

MON ANNIVERSAIRE
Leçon 1
"Les Nombres"

Vocabulaire

Comptez	Quinze
Count	*15*
Les chiffres	Seize
Numbers	*16*
Onze	Dix-sept
11	*17*
Douze	Dix-huit
12	*18*
Treize	Dix-neuf
13	*19*
Quatorze	Vingt
14	*20*

GREETINGS, REVISION

After everyone has greeted each other with **"Bonjour!"**, or **"Salut!"**, revise the **numbers from 1 – 10**. Introduce a number **song** or a game (see the Activités section on the next page). Follow the song counting with your fingers in the air.
The children usually like to copy this action.
Once you are sure that the children understand these numbers, further numbers can be learned.

Teaching Ideas

Materials: Number flashcards from page 30

Tell the children that they are going to learn how to count up to 20 in French. Ask them to **stand in a line** and count them out loud, ask the children to join in. **Repeat this a few times** so that the children hear the numbers clearly.
While the children are still standing, hand each of them a **flash card from 1 – 20** which **they hold up saying the number out loud in sequence**. Again practise this a few times.

Now the children **form a circle** still holding their flash cards. Tell them that now they are going to **swap their card** with another person in the circle as follows:-

The **teacher calls out** for example: **"douze, change avec quatorze"** So the child holding **flash card 12** has to go over to the child holding **flash card 14 and swap his / her card.**
The game becomes more exciting when the children have learnt the numbers so the game can then pick up pace.
See also the game **"Salade de Fruits"** in the Activités section page 8.

 Cocorico Books © Zara Mercer & Margaret Mckee 2009   **Vingt-huit**

"LES NOMBRES"

Mon anniversaire

"Loto des nombres"

Materials:	Photocopies of the Loto boards page 31-32
	Counters or pencils (optional)

Each child or team is given a board. The **teacher calls out the numbers** at the bottom of the page (in the style of Bingo). The children then **either cross out the numbers** as they hear them or **cover them with counters**. The **first "full house" wins.** The winning child must shout out **"J'ai gangé"**

N.B. The winner must then call out his numbers in French for the teacher to check

"Frère Jacques"

In this song the lyrics of **Frère Jacques** have been **altered**, and replaced by the the **numbers 1 to 20**. **Sing this song** with the children to practise the numbers :-

Un, deux, trois,
Un, deux, trois,
Quatre, cinq, six,
Quatre, cinq, six,
Sept, huit, neuf, dix,
Sept, huit, neuf, dix,
Onze, douze, treize,
Onze, douze, treize,

Quatorze, quinze,
Quatorze, quinze,
Seize, dix-sept,
Seize, dix-sept,
Dix-huit, dix-neuf, vingt,
Dix-huit, dix-neuf, vingt,
Un, deux, trois,
Un, deux, trois.

 Cocorico Books © Zara Mercer & Margaret Mckee 2009

Vingt-neuf

~ Les Nombres ~

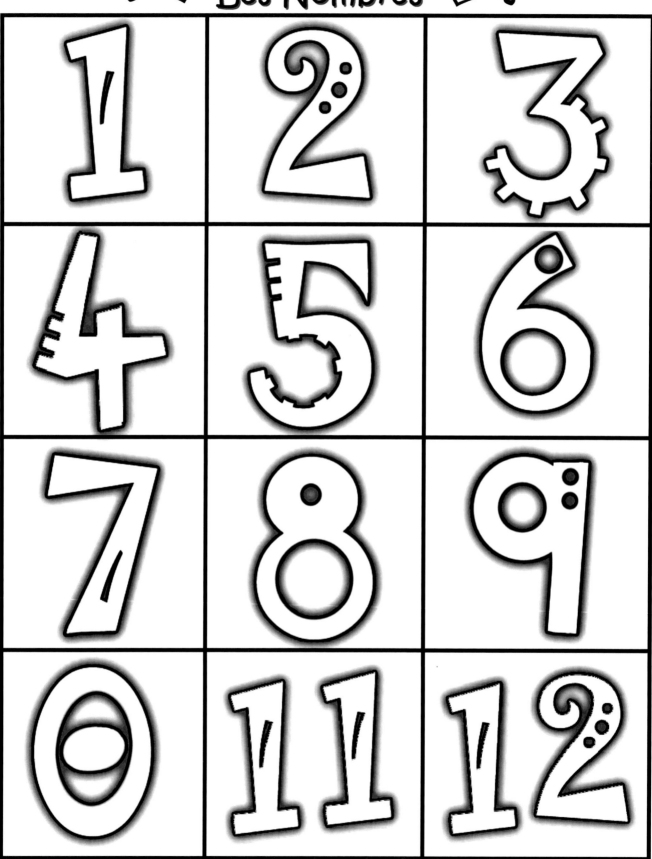

Cut out the pictures and enlarge for use as flashcards. Larger numbers can easily be made by putting one number in front of another (eg 25 would be 2 and 5)

 Cocorico Books © Zara Mercer & Margaret Mckee 2009

Trente

Loto des nombres 1

12	21	20
7	9	16
10	15	19

21	20	2
7	8	13
19	14	4

8	17	3
5	6	21
16	7	20

10	3	1
18	12	20
8	11	15

16	12	18
13	5	14
11	21	4

9	11	20
7	13	14
10	1	21

Un	Cinq	Douze	Quinze	Onze	Seize	Dix-sept
Quatorze	Neuf	Vingt-et-un	Deux	Huit	Quatre	Dix-neuf
Treize	Sept	Dix	Vingt	Trois	Dix-huit	Six

Photocopy, cut out, and distribute the loto boards. One loto board per player / group.
Call out the numbers in French as shown above

 Cocorico Books © Zara Mercer & Margaret Mckee 2009

Trente et un

Loto des nombres 2

2	19	20
17	8	13
6	10	1

21	10	2
4	9	16
19	13	5

18	12	19
3	17	6
14	13	20

21	14	15
11	13	4
20	1	16

18	17	19
5	6	20
8	13	12

15	10	20
9	13	11
19	3	2

Un	Cinq	Douze	Quinze	Onze	Seize	Dix-sept
Quatorze	Neuf	Vingt-et-un	Deux	Huit	Quatre	Dix-neuf
Treize	Sept	Dix	Vingt	Trois	Dix-huit	Six

Photocopy, cut out, and distribute the loto boards. One loto board per player / group.
Call out the numbers in French as shown above

 Cocorico Books © Zara Mercer & Margaret Mckee 2009

Trente-deux

Mots Mêlés

Les Nombres

```
Q L Z N P P I T B B H G M V A
I S A E D V C X R Z I S T Z D
F U N Y M F S X Z O O C W U S
M P Z N D I X J G P I Z G E C
L D P Y B W C U K T U S L D I
I E E I H Q Y C Y K H U I T N
Z O Q I C M X P N A D W L X Q
L N S I G M H Y W P J S I D H
N Z P C N B Y Q D O U Z E T O
Y E Q S B G D U Y W U J P K W
Y U U D Q T Q A W D L E F L T
S J D F E J C T S B S A Y B K
W Y P R X U Q R P R J K A H Y
P A A W U S X E H J R G H J R
I B N I M O G M D L J B P O S
```

un	cinq	neuf
deux	six	dix
trois	sept	onze
quatre	huit	douze

Trente-trois

Mon Anniversaire
Leçon 2
"Les jours de la semaine"

Vocabulaire

Lundi *Monday*	**Samedi** *Saturday*	**Vingt-deux** *22*	**Vingt-sept** *27*
Mardi *Tuesday*	**Dimanche** *Sunday*	**Vingt-trois** *23*	**Vingt-huit** *28*
Mercredi *Wednesday*	**La semaine** *The week*	**Vingt-quatre** *24*	**Vingt-neuf** *29*
Jeudi *Thursday*	**Le weekend** *The weekend*	**Vingt-cinq** *25*	**Trente** *30*
Vendredi *Friday*	**Vingt-et-un** *21*	**Vingt-six** *26*	**Trente-et-un** *31*

Greetings, Revision

After greeting the class ask several of the children:-

"Ça va? / Ça va bien? / Ça va mal?"

Revise numbers 1 – 20 : **bounce a ball** several times and ask the children to guess the number of bounces.
Ask a child to **count the class** and tell you the number present, or simply ask a few of the children to come to the front to count. Alternatively, use the number flashcards page 30 to revise counting.

Teaching Ideas

Materials: Flashcards of "Les Jours" page 36

Explain to the children that they are going to learn the days of the week: **"Les jours de la semaine"**.

Say the names of the days out loud in sequence.
Encourage everyone to repeat them with you. Repeat this exercise 3 times.

Copy on card a set of "Les Jours" flashcards from page 36, cut them out into cards and shuffle them.
Each child in turn must rearrange the cards in the correct order as fast as they can. To make the activity more exciting, use a stopwatch.

The children are now going to learn some more numbers. Count out loud to the class up to 31.
Once the children have heard the bigger numbers a few times, call out a few numbers in French for the children to translate into English.

Then repeat the exercise, this time the children must translate the numbers called from English into French (more difficult).

Write a few numbers on the board, for the children to read out loud in French.

Alternatively, the children go up to the board and the teacher must tell the child what number to write in French.

Cocorico Books © Zara Mercer & Margaret Mckee 2009

"LES JOURS DE LA SEMAINE"

Mon anniversaire

"Treize la bombe"

| Materials: Ball / beanbag |

The children form a **circle**. **A ball is thrown from one child to another** while **counting** aloud **from 1 – 13**: for example, the first child to catch the ball says **"un"** and then he/she **throws it to another** who says **"deux"**. This continues until **"treize"** is reached. The child who catches the ball **on that number is out**.
Play continues starting again with **"un"** and ending with **"treize"**. Several rounds are played until one child is left in the circle.

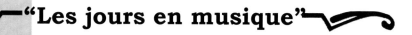

"Les jours en musique"

| Materials: Flashcards of "Les Jours" flashcards page 36 |
| CD player (French Music) |

Scatter the flashcards face down around the room. **Play a French song**. Stop the music, the children have to run and **stand next to a facedown flashcard of their choice**.
A day of the week is selected and called out e.g. **"Vendredi"**. The flashcards are turned over and **those standing next to "Vendredi" are out**. The flashcards are placed face down again and the game continues until one child is left.

"Le Facteur"
(the postman)

| Materials: Envelopes (4 per child) |
| Cardboard box (postbox) |

Write a day of the week on each envelope. Shuffle them up and give 4 envelopes to each child (It is ok if a child has 'doubles' of the same day)
The teacher or a child can be **"Le facteur"** (the postman).
"Le facteur" stands at one end of the room holding the "postbox" and **calls out a day of the week**. The children, standing at the other end of the room, **run to the postbox and post their corresponding letter.** The first child to post all his/her envelopes wins the game. (If a player has 2 envelopes with the same day of the week, only 1 of those can be posted at a time)

-36- Les jours

la semaine	lundi
mardi	mercredi
jeudi	vendredi
samedi	dimanche

Cut out the squares and enlarge for use as flashcards

Cocorico Books © Zara Mercer & Margaret Mckee 2009

Trente-six

Mots Mêlés

Les Jours

K	P	B	N	L	L	D	D	I	H	T	U	O	F	A
S	I	A	W	X	F	Y	I	J	L	U	N	D	I	X
V	G	N	C	O	V	I	V	B	D	N	Y	C	G	I
O	D	I	M	A	N	C	H	E	L	G	E	U	W	K
M	N	L	C	L	F	Y	G	Q	N	Z	T	P	I	N
S	A	M	E	D	I	C	Y	C	Z	D	G	V	H	J
B	N	R	D	N	O	D	L	D	A	X	R	P	N	E
P	B	I	D	F	O	T	E	E	L	W	I	E	X	U
N	W	J	Y	I	I	W	K	W	B	G	N	X	D	D
C	L	O	I	Z	U	N	E	C	E	G	R	L	Q	I
C	G	U	M	E	R	C	R	E	D	I	W	V	C	H
I	R	R	N	G	R	Y	H	I	K	I	A	D	Z	Q
E	C	L	J	D	W	K	J	L	J	E	E	A	T	C
L	S	E	M	A	I	N	E	T	R	E	N	T	R	J
S	Z	N	S	O	N	U	O	X	P	R	Z	D	N	I

(le) jour   mardi   samedi
(le) weekend   mercredi   dimanche
(la) semaine   jeudi
lundi   vendredi

Trente-sept

MON ANNIVERSAIRE
Leçon 3
"Les mois"

Vocabulaire

Les mois *the months*	mai *May*	octobre *October*
janvier *January*	juin *June*	novembre *November*
février *February*	juillet *July*	décembre *December*
mars *March*	août *August*	
avril *April*	septembre *September*	

GREETINGS, REVISION

After greeting each other and asking **"Ça va?"**, revise the numbers from **1 – 31** and ask the children if they can remember what **"Quel âge as- tu?"** means.
You may need to practise this again (see Toi et Moi Leçon 3 page 7)

Teaching Ideas

Materials: Flashcards of "Les Mois" page 42

Explain to the class that they are going to learn how to say the **date of their birthday.** To do this they need to learn **all of the months in French**. First, read them out using "Les Mois" flashcards page 42, repeat with the children at least 3 times. Go around the class **giving each child a month** to say starting with **"janvier"**. (If you have more than 12 in the class start the sequence again.)

Tell them the date of your birthday eg **"Mon anniversaire est le 23 juillet"**. Now introduce the question; **"Quelle est la date de ton anniversaire?"**
Ask each child to think about the date of their birthday.

Now you can help the children to answer the question in French beginning with:-

"Mon anniversaire est le ..."

For example the **18th July** will be **"Mon anniversaire est le dix-huit juillet"**.

The children can get into **pairs** and practise a **short role-play**. One child has to start by asking **"Quelle est la date de ton anniversaire?"** and the other answers with **"Mon anniversaire est le….."**. The teacher will need to circulate around the room helping each pair.

N.B. The first is "Le premier" of the month

 Cocorico Books © Zara Mercer & Margaret Mckee 2009

"LES MOIS"

"La fête"

In France every child has a **second birthday** called **"la fête"**

Each child shares this second birthday with the day of the Saint who has the same name.

For example Jessica was born on 20th February and St. Jessica's day is the 4th November ("La Fête"). In this way Jessica would celebrate her **"Anniversaire"** on 20th February and her **"Fête"** on 4th November.

Every day in France there is an announcement on the television, radio and in the newspapers informing the public which Saint's day will be celebrated the following day.

Using the "Calendrier des Saints et des prénoms" page 40-41, find the date of each child's "Fête" according to their first name.

If a child's name does not appear on the calendar try using their middle name.

Failing that, suggest that the child chooses his or her own Saint.

Grégory 3 sept
Guénolé 3 mars
Guillaume 10 jan
Guillemette 10 jan
Gustave 7 oct
Guy 12 juin
Gwendoline 14 oct
Gwaldys 29 mars

H
Harold 1 nov
Harry 13 juil
Helene 18 aout
Henri 13 juil
Henriette 13 juil
Herbert 20 mars
Hermes 28 aout
Herve 17 juin
Hilaire 13 janv
Hilda 17 november
Honore 16 mai
Hugues 1 avril
Hyacinthe 17 aout

I
Ida 13 avril
Ignace 17 oct
Igor 5 juin
Inès 10 sept
Ingrid 2 sept
Irène 5 avril
Irénée 28 juin
Iris 4 septembre
Irma 9 juillet
Isaac 20 décembre
Isabelle 22 février
Isidore 4 avril
Ivan 24 juin

J
Jacinthe 30 jan
Jack 24 juin
Jacky 3 mai
Jacqueline 8 fév
James 25 juil
Jasmine 5 oct
Jean (l'Apotre) 27 déc
Jean-Batiste 24 juin
Jean 23 oct
Jean(de Damas)8 mars
Jeanne 8 mai
Jérémie 1 mai
Jérôme 30 sept
Jessica 4 nov
Joël 13 juil
Johanne 30 mai
John 24 juin
Johnny 27 déc
Joseph 19 mars
Joséphine 19 mars
Josiane 19 mars
Judith 5 mai

Jules 12 avril
Julie 8 avril
Julien 2 août
Justine 12 mars

K
Karen 7 nov
Karine 7 nov
Karine 24 mars
Katy 25 nov
Kévin 3 juin

L
Laetitia 18 août
Lambert 17 sept
Laure 10 août
Laurent 10 août
Laurence 10 août
Léa 22 mars
Leïla 22 mars
Léon 10 nov
Léonard 6 nov
Léonce 18 juin
Léontine 10 nov
Léopold 15 nov
Leslie 17 nov
Liliane 4 juil
Lily 17 nov
Linda 28 nov
Line 20 oct
Lionel 10 nov
Lise 17 nov
Loïc 25 août
Lola 15 sept
Lolita 15 sept
Lore 25 juin
Louis (France)25 août
Louis-Marie 28 avril
Louise 15 mars
Loup 29 juil
Luc 18 oct
Lucas 18 oct
Lucette 13 déc
Lucie 13 déc
Lucien 8 jan
Lucienne 8 jan
Lucille 16 fév
Lucrère 15 mars
Ludmilla 16 sept
Ludovic 25 août
Ludwig 25 août
Lydie 3 oct

M
Madeleine 22 juil
Nadette 18 fév
Maël 24 mai
Magali 20 juil
Maggy 20 juil
Maïté 7 juin
Manuel 25 déc
Marc 25 avril

Marcel 16 jan
Marcelle 31 jan
Marcellin 6 avril
Marguerite 20 juil
Marianne 9 juil
Marie 15 août
Marielle 15 août
Marie-Madeleine 22 juil
Marie-Thérèse 7 juin
Marilyne 15 août
Marina 20 juil
Marinette 20 juil
Marion 15 août
Marius 19 jan
Marjorie 20 juil
Marlène 15 août
Marthe 298 juil
Martial 30 juin
Martin 11 nov
Martine 30 jan
Marylise 15 août
Maryse 15 août
Maryvonne 15 août
Marthilde 14 mars

Matthias 14 mai
Mathieu 21 sept
Maud 14 mars
Maurice 22 sept
Mauricette 22 sept
Maxime 14 avril
Mélanie 26 jan
Michel 29 sept
Mickaël 29 sept
Mireille 15 août
Monique 27 août
Muriel 15 août
Myriam 15 août
Myrtille 5 oct

N
Nadège 18 sept
Nadette 18 fév
Nadia 18 sept
Nadine 18 nov
Narcisse 29 oct
Natacha 26 avril
Nathalie 27 juil
Nelly 18 août

Nestor 26 fév
Nicolas 6 déc
Nicole 6 mars
Nina 14 jan
Ninon 15 nov
Noël 25 déc
Noëmie 21 août
Norbert 6 juin

O
Octave 20 nov
Odette 20 avril
Odile 14 déc
Olga 11 juil
Olive 5 mars
Olivia 5 mars
Olivier 12 juil
Oscar 3 fév

P
Paquerette 5 oct
Pascal 17 mai
Patrice 17 mars
Patricia 17 mars
Patrick 17 mars
Paul 29 juin

Paula 26 jan
Paule 26 jan
Paulette 26 jan
Paulin 11 jan
Pauline 26 jan
Pélagie 8 oct
Perrette 31 mai
Perrine 31 mai
Pervenche 5 oct
Peter 29 juin
Pétronille 31 mai
Philippe 3 mai
Philomène 13 août
Pierre 29 juin
Pierrette 31 mai
Priscilla 16 jan
Prosper 25 juin
Prudence 6 mai

Q
Quentin 31 oct

R
Rachel 15 jan
Rachilde 23 nov

Raïssa 5 sept
Raoul 7 juil
Raphaël 29 sept
Raymond 7 jan
Rebecca 23 mars
Régine 7 sept
Régis 16 juin
Reine 7 sept
Rémi 15 jan
Renaud 17 sept
René 19 oct
Richard 3 avril
Rita 22 mai
Robert 30 avril
Roberte 30 avril
Robin 30 avril
Roch 16 août
Rodolphe 21 juin
Rodrigue 13 mars
Roger 30 déc
Roland 15 sept
Rolande 13 mai
Romain 28 fév
Romaric 10 déc
Roméo 25 fév
Romuald 19 juin
Rosalie 4 sept
Rose 23 août
Roseline 17 jan
Rosette 23 août
Rosine 11 mars

S
Sabine 29 août
Sabrina 29 août
Salomon 25 juin
Samson 28 juil
Samuel 20 août
Samy 20 août
Sandrine 2 avril
Sarah 9 oct
Sébastien 20 jan
Ségolène 24 juil
Serge 7 oct
Séverine 27 nov
Sheila 22 nov
Sibille 9 oct
Simon 28 oct
Simone 28 oct
Solange 10 mai
Solenne 17 oct
Sonia 18 sept
Sophie 25 mai
Stéphane 26 déc
Suzanne 11 août
Suzy 11 août
Sylvain 4 mai
Sylvestre 31 déc
Sylviane 5 nov
Sylvie 5 nov

T
Tamara 1 mai
Tanguy 19 nov
Tania 12 jan
Teddy 5 jan
Térésa 15 oct
Théodore 9 nov
Théophile 20 déc
Thérèse 15 oct
Thérèse oct
Thibaut 8 juil
Thierry 1 juil
Thomas 3 juil
Tino 3 juil
Toinon 28 fév
Toussaint 1 nov
Tudal 1 déc
Tudi 9 mai

U
Ulrich 10 juil
Ursula 21 oct

V
Valentin 14 fév
Valentine 25 juil
Valérie 28 avril
Valéry 1 Avril
Vanessa 4 fév
Venceslas 28 sept
Véronique 4 fév
Victor 21 juil

X
Xavier 3 déc
Xavière 22 déc

Y
Yann 24 juin
Yannick 24 juin
Yoann 24 juin
Yolande 11 juin
Yvan 24 juin
Yves 19 mai
Yvette 13 jan
Yvon 19 mai
Yvonne 19 mai

Z
Zacharie 5 nov
Zélie 17 oct
Zénaïde 11 oct
Zéphirin 26 déc
Zita 27 avril
Zoé 2 mai

Cherche ton prénom dans le calendrier pour la date de ta fête.

Cocorico Books © Zara Mercer & Margaret Mckee 2009

Calendrier des Saints et des Prénoms

Find your first name (or middle name) in the calendar for the date of your "fête"!

A
Aaron 1 juil
Abel 5 août
Abella 5 Août
Abraham 20 déc
Achille 12 mai
Adélaïde 16 déc
Adèle 24 déc
Adeline 20 oct
Adelphe 11 sept
Adolphe 30 juin
Adrien 8 sept
Adrienne 8 sept
Agathe 5 fév
Agnès 21 juin
Aimable 18 oct
Aimé 13 sept
Aimée 20 fév
Alain 9 sept
Alban 22 juin
Albéric 15 nov
Albert 15 nov
Alberte 15 nov
Albin 1 mars
Alexandra 22 avril
Alexandre 22 avril
Alexis 17 fév
Alfred 15 Août
Alice 16 déc
Alida 26 avril
Aline 20 oct
Alix 9 jan
Alphonse 1 août
Amand 6 fév
Amandine 9 juil
Amaury 15 jan
Ambroise 7 déc
Amélie 19 sept
Amour 9 août
Anaïs 26 juil
Anastasie 10 mars
Anatole 3 fév
André 30 nov
Ange 5 mai
Angèle 27 jan
Angélique 27 jan
Anicet 17 avril
Anita 26 juil
Anna 26 juil
Annabelle 26 juil
Annette 26 juil
Annick 26 juil
Annie 26 juil
Anouchka 26 juil
Anouck 26 juil
Anselme 21 avril
Anthelme 26 juin
Anthony 17 jan
Antoine 5 juil
Antoine de P 13 juin
Antoinette 5 juil
Antonin 2 mai
Apolline 9 fév
Apollinaire 12 sept
Ariane 18 sept
Arielle 1 oct
Aristide 31 août
Arlette 17 juil
Armand 23 déc
Armel 16 août
Arnaud 10 fév
Arnold 14 août
Arsène 19 juil
Arthur 15 nov
Astrid 27 nov
Aubin 1 mars
Aude 18 nov
Audrey 23 juin
Auguste 29 fév
Augustin 27 mai
Augustine 13 nov
Aurèle 15 oct
Aurélie 15 oct
Aurélien 16 juin
Aurore 13 déc
Axelle 22 avril
Aymeric 24 nov

B
Babette 17 nov
Baptiste 24 juin
Barbara 4 déc
Barnabé 11 juin
Barnard 23 jan
Barthélemy 24 août
Basile 2 jan
Bastien 20 jan
Baudouin 17 oct
Béatrice 13 fév
Bénédicte 16 mars
Benjamin 31 mars
Benoît 11 juil
Benoît-Joseph 16 avril
Bérenger 26 mai
Bérénice 4 fév
Bernadette 18 fév
Bernard (de C.) 20 août
Bernard (de M.) 15 juin
Berthe 4 juil
Bertiulle 6 nov
Bettina 17 nov
Betty 17 nov
Bienvenue 30 oct
Blaise 3 fév
Blanche 3 oct
Blandine 2 juin
Bluette 5 oct
Boris 2 mai
Brice 13 nov
Brigitte 23 juil
Bruno 6 oct

C
Camille 14 juil
Candide 3 oct
Capucine 5 oct
Carine 7 nov
Carlos 4 nov
Carmen 16 juil
Carole 17 juil
Caroline 17 juil
Casimir 15 mars
Catherine 25 nov
Cécile 22 nov
Cédric 7 jan
Céleste 14 oct
Célia 22 nov
Céline 21 oct
César 26 août
Chantal 12 déc
Charles 2 mars
Charlotte 17 juil
Charly 4 nov
Christel(le) 24 juil
Christian 12 nov
Christiane 24 juil
Christiane 12 nov
Christine 24 juil
Christophe 21 août
Claire 11 août
Clara 11 août
Clarisse 12 août
Claude 15 fév
Claudette 15 fév
Claudie 15 fév
Claudine 15 fév
Clémence 21 mars
Clément 23 nov
Clémentine 23 nov
Clotilde 4 juin
Clovis 25 août
Colette 6 mars
Colin 6 déc
Colombe 31 déc
Conrad 26 nov
Constance 8 avril
Constant 23 sept
Coralie 18 mai
Corentin (e) 12 déc
Corinne 18 mai
Cyprien 16 sep
Cyrille 18 mars

D
Dahlia 5 oct
Daisy 16 nov
Damien 26 sept
Daniel 11 déc
Danielle 11 déc
Dany 11 déc
David 29 déc
Davy 20 sept
Déborah 21 sept
Delphine 26 nov
Denis 9 oct
Denise 15 mai
Désiré 8 mai
Diane 9 juin
Didier 23 mai
Dimitri 26 oct
Dolorès 15 sept
Dominique 8 août
Donatien 24 mai
Dorine 9 nov
Doris 6 fév
Dorothée 6 fév

E
Edgar 8 juil
Edith 16 sept
Edmond 20 nov
Edouard 5 jan
Edwige 16 oct
Eglantine 23 août
Elé onore 25 juin
Elfried 8 déc
Elie 20 juil
Eliane 4 juil
Eliette 20 juil
Elisabeth 17 nov
Elise 17 nov
Elisée 14 juin
Ella 1 fév
Elodie 22 oct
Eloi 1 déc
Elsa 17 nov
Elvire 16 juil
Emeline 17 oct
Emeric 4 nov
Emile 22 mai
Emilie 19 sept
Emilien 12 nov
Emilienne 5 jan
Emma 19 avril
Emmanuel 25 déc
Eric 18 mai
Erich 18 mai
Erika 18 mai
Ernest 7 nov
Ernestine 7 nov
Estelle 11 mai
Esther 1 juil
Etienne 26 déc
Eudes (Jean) 19 août
Eugène 13 juil
Eugénie 7 fév
Eva 6 sept
Evelyne 6 sept
Evelyne 27 déc
Evrard 14 août

F
Fabienne 20 jan
Fabrice 22 août
Fanny 26 déc
Félicie 7 mars
Félicien 9 juil
Félicité 7 mars
Félix 12 fév
Ferdinand 30 mai
Fernand 27 juin
Fidèle 24 avril
Firmin 11 oct
Flavie 7 mai
Flavien 18 fév
Fleur 5 oct
Flora 24 nov
Florence 1 déc
Florent 4 juil
Florentin 4 juil
Florian 4 mai
Florine 1 mai
France 9 mars
Francine 9 mars
Francis 4 oct
Franck 4 oct
François 24 jan
François (d'Assise) 4 oct
François-Xavier 3 déc
Françoise 9 mars
Françoise 12 déc
Freddy 18 juil
Frédéric 18 juil
Frédérique 18 juil
Fulbert 10 avril

G
Gabin 19 fév
Gabriel(le) 29 sept
Gaby 29 sept
Gaël 17 déc
Gaëlle 17 déc
Gaëtan 7 août
Gaspard 28 déc
Gaston 6 fév
Geneviève 3 jan
Geoffroy 8 nov
Georges 23 avril
Georgia 15 fév
Gérald 5 déc
Géraldine 5 déc
Gerard 3 oct
Germaine 15 juin
Gertrude 16 nov
Ghislain 10 oct
Gilbert 7 juin
Gilberte 11 août
Gilles 1 sept
Gina 21 juin
Gisèle 7 mai
Godefroy 8 nov
Gonzague 21 juin
Gontran 28 mars
Grégoire 3 sept

Les mois

janvier	février	mars
avril	mai	juin
juillet	août	septembre
octobre	novembre	décembre

Cut out the squares and enlarge for use as flashcards

 Cocorico Books © Zara Mercer & Margaret Mckee 2009

Quarante-deux

loto des mois 1

Janvier	Juillet	Lundi
Dimanche	Mai	Novembre
Vendredi	Mars	Septembre

Août	Avril	Janvier
Vendredi	Mois	Lundi
Juin	Mercredi	Décembre

Juin	Mars	Mai
Mois	Août	Juillet
Novembre	Jeudi	Janvier

Février	Jeudi	Mardi
Dimanche	Juin	Décembre
Samedi	Avril	Octobre

Mai	Novembre	Mois
Samedi	Mars	Septembre
Lundi	Juillet	Février

Mardi	Décembre	Juin
Février	Octobre	Vendredi
Septembre	Dimanche	Jeudi

January	October	Monday	April	June
July	March	December	August	Tuesday
Friday	September	February	Wednesday	Saturday
Month	Thursday	November	May	Sunday

Photocopy, cut out, and distribute the loto boards. One loto board per player / group. Call out the words in English as shown above

Cocorico Books © Zara Mercer & Margaret Mckee 2009

Quarante-trois

Loto des mois 2

Décembre	Jeudi	Mois
Dimanche	Juin	Février
Janvier	Avril	Août

Mai	Vendredi	Jeudi
Septembre	Juin	Lundi
Mercredi	Juillet	Avril

Février	Mardi	Mois
Juin	Samedi	Lundi
Octobre	Dimanche	Mois

Janvier	Août	Mai
Octobre	Septembre	Mois
Mercredi	Novembre	Jeudi

Mars	Mercredi	Septembre
Juillet	Dimanche	Janvier
Novembre	Avril	Vendredi

Décembre	Février	Mars
Mai	Août	Mardi
Samedi	Mars	Lundi

January	October	Monday	April	June
July	March	December	August	Tuesday
Friday	September	February	Wednesday	Saturday
Month	Thursday	November	May	Sunday

Photocopy, cut out, and distribute the loto boards. One loto board per player / group. Call out the words in English as shown above

 Cocorico Books © Zara Mercer & Margaret Mckee 2009

Quarante-quatre

Mots Mêlés

Les mois

I	N	A	L	J	Z	L	A	A	F	R	S	J	B	Y
Q	G	Y	U	V	D	W	O	D	A	Q	G	U	C	V
O	E	L	B	M	T	G	U	R	C	L	W	I	K	G
M	C	I	C	Q	V	Q	T	S	J	E	A	L	R	D
N	V	T	B	X	G	W	E	O	F	E	D	L	X	E
M	L	U	O	R	I	P	W	B	O	R	E	E	E	C
A	A	I	Q	B	T	A	R	S	Y	V	C	T	B	E
N	J	I	Q	E	R	F	B	C	J	U	I	N	V	M
L	L	J	M	L	X	E	I	U	A	E	L	V	F	B
B	U	B	D	X	S	V	E	Z	C	E	P	J	O	R
B	R	E	C	I	F	R	Y	C	M	A	U	T	N	E
E	P	V	T	E	P	I	F	Z	A	G	V	B	X	O
C	B	J	N	O	V	E	M	B	R	E	O	R	R	B
J	A	N	V	I	E	R	U	R	S	H	S	R	I	H
Q	X	L	L	M	L	S	M	V	N	P	X	J	L	L

janvier   mai   septembre
février   juin   octobre
mars   juillet   novembre
avril   août   décembre

DANS MA CLASSE
Leçon 1
"La Classe"

Vocabulaire

Dans ma classe il y a ...
In my class there is ...

Un Tableau
A board

Une table
A table

Une chaise
A chair

Un livre
A book

Une porte
A door

Une fenêtre
A window

Un bureau
A desk

Un placard
A cupboard

Un cahier
A notebook

Touche !
Touch (it!)

GREETINGS, REVISION

After the usual greetings revise any of the following:-
a) les couleurs - "**Quelle est ta couleur préférée?**"
b) Les mois - "**Quelle est la date ... d'aujourd'hui?**" or " **... de ton anniversaire**"
c) Mix up a set of **"Les Mois"** flashcards page 42, the children then take it in turn to put them in order.
d) Do the same with "Les Jours" flashcards page 36

Use a stop watch to make the activities more fun for the children

Teaching Ideas

Materials: 'Objets de la classe' flashcards page 48
Large labels

Bonjour les enfants Cocorico!

For this topic use the flashcards or find the objects in the classroom itself.
Go through the names of the objects, with the children.
Using a felt pen, you can make **labels in French** and stick them on to each object around the classroom (the children can help).
Walk around the class **pointing** to and **naming** the items **in French**, the **children repeat after you.**
When the children have a good understanding of the vocabulary, play the following game.

Memory Game

Use the flashcards as prompts, alternatively point at the objects around the class room.

   Teacher - "**Dans ma classe il y a un bureau.**"
   Child 1 - "**Dans ma classe il y a un bureau et une table.**"
   Child 2 - "**Dans ma classe il y a un bureau et une table et un placard.**"

The game continues like this until all the vocabulary has been used.

Cocorico Books © Zara Mercer & Margaret Mckee 2009

Quarante-six

"LA CLASSE"

Dans ma classe

"Touche à tout"

In the classroom, **clear any obstacles so that the children can run around freely**. Using the vocabulary listed below, explain to the children that when an object is called out they must **go and touch it** e.g. **"touchez un livre rouge, une table"** etc. The last child to touch the object is out.
Continue this until a winner is found.

- une table   - une chaise   - un livre   - un tableau
- une porte   - une fenêtre   - un placard   - un bureau

"Salade de fruits"

Materials: Chairs

Arrange enough chairs in a circle for the whole class except for one child who will stand in the centre. Use the new vocabulary on page 46 to play **"Salade"** as explained on page 8

Cocorico Books © Zara Mercer & Margaret Mckee 2009

Les Objets de la classe

Qu'est ce qu'il y a dans la classe?

Put the correct numbers in the picture above using the list below
(the first one has been done for you)

(1)[eg]   Une table ✓
(2)   Une chaise
(3)   Une porte
(4)   Une fenêtre
(5)   Un placard
(6)   Des crayons
(7)   Une règle
(8)   Une gomme
(9)   Un stylo
(10)   Des fleurs
(11)   Un livre
(12)   Le T_____

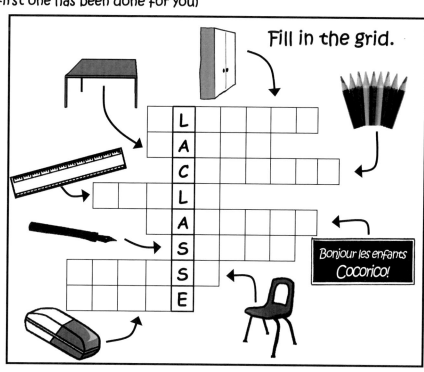

Fill in the grid.

Quarante-neuf

DANS MA CLASSE
— Leçon 2 —
"Dans ma trousse il y a..."

Vocabulaire

Dans ma trousse il y a ...
In my pencil case there is ...

Des crayons de couleur
Coloured pencils

Un taille-crayon *A pencil sharpener*	**Une gomme** *A rubber*
Un stylo *A pen*	**Un crayon** *A pencil*
Une trousse *A pencil case*	**La colle** *Glue*
Une règle *A ruler*	**Un cartable** *A satchel*

GREETINGS, REVISION

Review all the vocabulary from Leçon 1. Play a quick round of the "**Jeu de Mémoiré**" on page 16.

Start off by pointing to an object, and saying e.g. "**Dans ma classe il y a une porte**". The next child repeats the sentence and adds another word.

Alternatively a variation of the game "**touche**" could be played. Choose a child. Call out "**Touche une table**" (or other vocabulary that has been covered) and the chosen child must run to a table and touch it. A more energetic activity would be to get the whole class to run and touch the objects called out.

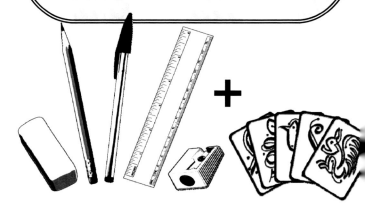

Teaching Ideas

Materials:	Set of 'Les objets de la classe' Flashcards page 48
	Pencil case containing stationary

Cut out flashcards or use real objects to demonstrate the vocabulary above. If using real objects, the teacher could hold up "**Une trousse**" and repeat the names of the various objects while putting them back in the pencil case, for example "**Dans la trousse il y a une gomme**". The children might like to take turns at doing this.

Alternatively the children can describe in French what is inside their own pencil case. This is a good opportunity to go extend the vocabulary eg
"**Il y a .. de l'argent**", "**... des étiquettes**" etc.

Another activity is to **place all of the objects** (or flashcards) on the floor or on a table. The children then pick up the objects one by one and name them in French.
To make this more exciting, one object can be discretely removed and the children have to guess which item is missing.

"DANS MA TROUSSE IL Y A"

"C'est Caché"

| Materials: | Pencil case objects |

Place the objects on a table and tell the children to **repeat the names using the definite article** - la règle, le stylo etc. Divide the class into **2 or 3 teams**. A member of team 1 looks away from the table while **the other team removes and hides two of the objects**. The child then turns back to face the table and tries to **guess which two objects are missing.** The next turn then goes to a member of team 2. (They must hide objects for team 3 to guess etc) Continue like this until each team member has had a turn at guessing.
More objects can be added to the table 'sneakily' if the class enjoys this game. This not only makes the lesson more fun but also introduces the names of a few extra objects.

"Les objets en musique"

| Materials: | "Les Objets de la classe" flashcards page 48
CD player |

a) **Scatter** the flashcards **picture side up** around the room. **Play a French song** on the cd player. **Stop the music**. The children have to **run and stand** next to a flashcard of their choice. One of the objects is **called out by the teacher** and the children standing next to that card **are out**. The game continues like this until a winner is found.
b) Scatter the flashcards **picture side down**. Then play the game as in (a) but the teacher calls out the object while the music is still playing. When the children do stop, they must then turn over the card they have chosen. In this faster variation, only the children standing by the card called out stay in the game.

"Jeu de mémoire"

| Materials: Two sets of "Les Objets de la classe" flashcards page 48 |

a. **Spread the flashcards face down** on the table. One child **turns** a **card over** and **names it in French**. If they are correct, **they keep the card**, if incorrect, the teacher says the name and the card is **replaced**. A second child has a turn and the game continues like this until all cards have been taken.
b. **Using 2 sets of flashcards** spread them out in the same way as explained above. This time each child **turns over 2 cards** and if the pictures match, the child keeps the pair. If they do not match, **both cards** are turned back **face down** and the next child plays. It is important that the children **name each card they turn over in French**.

Mots Mêlés

Dans mon Sac

M	D	W	S	F	Z	C	H	E	O	O	L	U	O	V
P	C	Y	F	H	R	S	D	T	L	N	O	C	L	P
B	G	F	P	A	C	O	L	L	E	G	S	V	Y	S
R	K	O	Y	H	O	K	K	V	R	D	É	D	T	A
Z	G	O	M	L	N	L	K	S	S	Y	W	R	S	C
Q	N	J	V	M	U	N	E	N	R	E	I	H	A	C
V	D	H	O	O	E	R	R	Q	Y	C	Z	A	C	R
C	D	G	R	P	A	Y	T	C	M	Z	U	T	K	W
H	A	W	I	L	W	L	Z	S	Q	Y	K	X	S	T
T	A	R	C	E	E	E	R	X	L	S	E	F	G	R
D	P	G	T	R	N	O	S	T	Q	L	R	J	S	O
B	Y	S	V	A	M	M	K	D	V	Y	W	M	Z	U
D	M	I	E	N	B	Z	W	N	G	O	B	J	O	S
I	L	B	V	W	M	L	K	L	L	X	A	K	K	S
U	K	H	X	D	B	S	E	V	Z	Z	P	I	H	E

(un) cahier   (une) gomme   (un) sac
(un) cartable   (un) livre   (un) stylo
(une) colle   (une) règle   (une) trousse
(un) crayon

Cocorico Books © Zara Mercer & Margaret Mckee 2009

Cinquante-deux

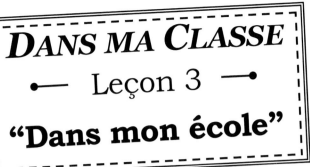

DANS MA CLASSE
Leçon 3
"Dans mon école"

GREETINGS, REVISION

Play a quick **"Qu'est-ce que c'est?"** game.

Pointing to objects around the room or items in a pencil case.

Vocabulaire

La salle de technologie
The IT room

Dans mon école il y a ...
In my school there is ...

La salle de musique
The music room

La salle de gym
The sports room/hall

La classe
The classroom

La bibliothèque
The library

La salle d'art
The art room

La piscine
The swimming pool

La cour
The playground

La cantine
The canteen

Le hall
The hall

La salle
The room

Teaching Ideas

Materials: One copy of the school plan "A l'école" page 55 for two children to share

The above vocabulary will help the children when naming school areas. Go through the school plan "A l'école", with the children naming all the rooms. You might want to make labels to stick around the school.

Play "Jeu de Mémoire" on page 16 starting **"Dans mon école il y a ..."**

Take the children around your school with a copy of the plan "A l'école".
Name the different areas of the school and use the stickers (if you have made them) to label different area.

Cocorico Books © Zara Mercer & Margaret Mckee 2009

Cinquante-trois

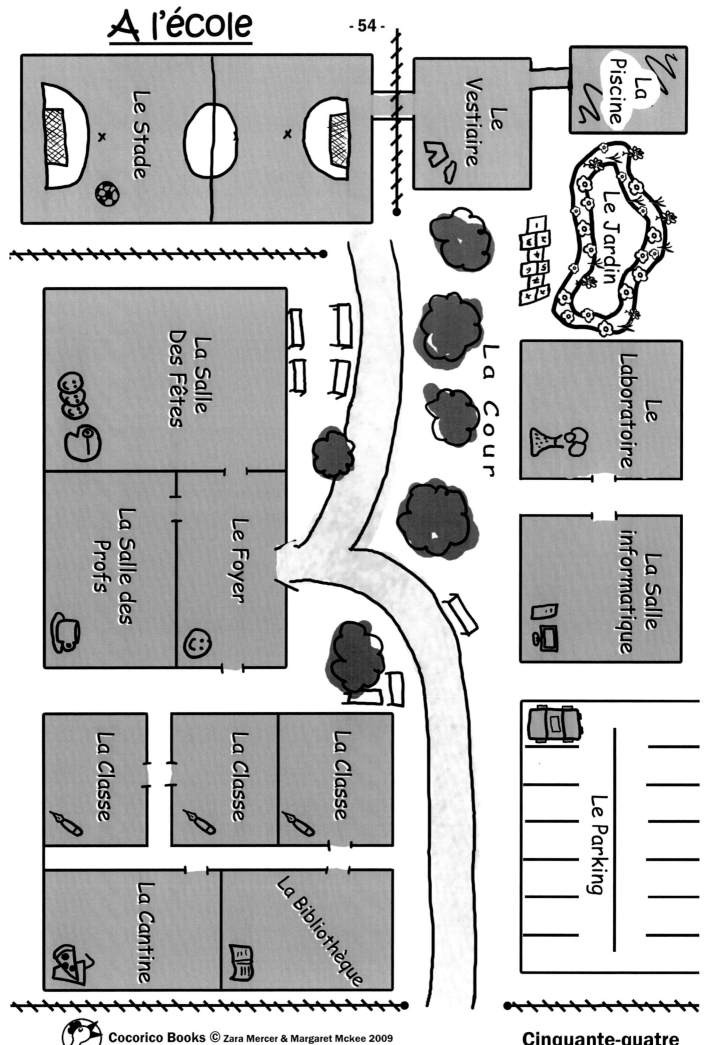

AU CAFÉ
Leçon 1
"Que désires-tu?"

Vocabulaire

Que désirez-vous?
What would you like? [polite form]

Que désires-tu?
What would you like? [informal]

Je voudrais
I would like

Un jus d'orange
An orange juice

Le café
The coffee shop

Un sandwich
A sandwich

Un coca
A coke

Une limonade
A lemonde

Merci
Thank you

Un gâteau
A cake

S'il vous plaît
If you please

Un café
A coffee

Un thé
A tea

Voici ...
Here/here is ...

GREETINGS, REVISION

Revise the **"Dans ma classe"** vocabulary, play a 5 minute warm-up exercise of **"Touche à tout"**.

Call out an object, the children must run and touch it.

Teaching Ideas

Materials: Enlarge and copy the "loto" food cards to use as flashcards page 57-58 (colour in if time)

Explain to the children that they are going to learn about **ordering food and drink in a café. Discuss** with the children some of the things you can eat and drink in a café in France.

Show them flashcards of the various food and drink items listed above and have the children **repeat** the **French words** after you.

Start the **following dialogue** with the children:

"Que désires - tu?"
"Je voudrais ... *[name of food]* , s'il vous plaît"

Once they have mastered this they are ready to practise a role-play with child 1 as the waiter and child 2 as the customer.

Child 1:- "Que désirez-vous, madame/monsieur/mademoiselle?"
Child 2:- "Je voudrais *un sandwich* et *un coca*, s'il vous plaît."
Child 1:- "Tout de suite Monsieur"

Cocorico Books © Zara Mercer & Margaret Mckee 2009   Cinquante-cinq

"QUE DÉSIRES - TU?"

"Que désirez-vous au café?"

Write some food words (*Vocabulaire* page 55) on the board or use flashcards for this exercise. Children **form a circle holding hands** with **1 child in the centre**.
The children walk to the left, moving the circle clockwise **while singing the first 3 lines of the song below.** After the 3rd line they stop moving and the child in the **centre** sings the **line in bold** and then **swaps places with another child in the circle of his/her choice.** The song continues

(to the tune of Skip to my Lou my Darling")

Que désirez-vous au café?
Que désirez-vous au café?
Que désirez-vous au café?
« Je voudrais un gâteau »

Je voudrais s'il vous plait.
Je voudrais s'il vous plait.
Je voudrais s'il vous plait.
« Je voudrais un gâteau. »

Que désirez -vous au café? (3 times)
« Je voudrais un sandwich. »

Je voudrais s'il vous plait (3 times)
« Je voudrais un sandwich. »

Que désirez-vous au café? (3 times)
« Je voudrais un coca. »

Je voudrais s'il vous plait (3 times)
« Je voudrais un coca. »

"Je voudrais …"
[Everyone joins in singing the last 3 lines.]

"Au café"

(advanced roleplay)

Materials:	Desks set up as café tables
	One copy of the menu per table page 63
	Tea-towel, note book, apron (for waiters)

Divide the class into small groups. Each group sits at a table. **Give each group a menu.** Read through it and explain any difficult vocabulary making sure the children pronounce the words correctly.
Choose **1 person in the group to be the "waiter"**. Initially the teacher is the **"Chef"**. Later a child can play the part. **Each** pupil in the group chooses **1 drink and 1 snack** from the menu and then gives his/her order to the waiter.
The waiter then in a **loud voice** calls out the orders to the Chef who is **standing a distance away from the groups (i.e. in the "kitchen")**. The Chef then repeats the order, **correcting any errors.**
This role-play can be acted out using basic props e.g. the waiter carries a tea-towel draped over one arm and holds a note book and pencil to take down the orders.

 Cocorico Books © Zara Mercer & Margaret Mckee 2009

~Au Café~

Loto au café .1

Vocab: Une Baguette. Des Céréales. Du Chocolat. Du Jus d'orange. Des Frites. Du Fromage. De la Confiture. Des Crêpes. Un Hamburger. De la Glace. Une Tarte aux Pommes. Un poulet. Un Croissant. Un Gâteau. Une Salade. Un Sandwich.

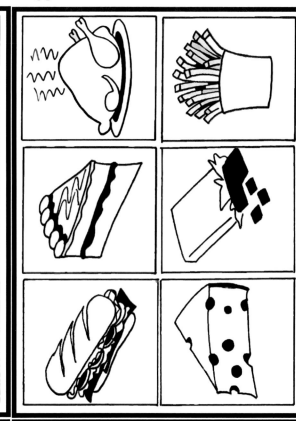

How to play

Copy and cut out two sets of the loto boards (loto au café 1 and 2). One for loto boards and the other to cut up into cards.

Distribute the loto boards, one per child/group.

Shuffle the set of cards and call out the first card in French e.g. "Du chocolat". A child who has "Du Chocolat" on his / her board calls out "ici!", pointing to the image.

He / she then receives the card and covers the image on their loto board, picture face down.

Cocorico Books © Zara Mercer & Margaret Mckee 2009

Cinquante-huit

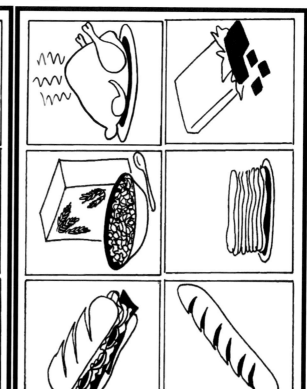

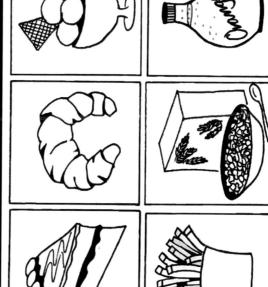

Vocab: Une Baguette. Des Céréales. Du Chocolat. Du Jus d'orange. Des Frites. Du Fromage. De la Confiture. Des Crêpes. Un Hamburger. De la Glace. Une Tarte aux Pommes. Un poulet. Un Croissant. Un Gâteau. Une Salade. Un Sandwich.

Loto au café 2

How to play

Copy and cut out two sets of the loto boards (loto au café 1 and 2). One for loto boards and the other to cut up into cards.

Distribute the loto boards, one per child/group.

Shuffle the set of cards and call out the first card in French e.g. **"Du chocolat"**. A child who has "Du Chocolat" on his / her board calls out "ici!", pointing to the image.

He / she then receives the card and covers the image on their loto board, picture face down.

Cocorico Books © Zara Mercer & Margaret Mckee 2009

Cinquante-neuf

AU CAFÉ
Leçon 2
"Je voudrais..."

GREETINGS, REVISION

Review all the vocabulary from in **Leçon 1** by holding up the **flashcards** one at a time and getting the children to **name** the various food/drink items. You may have to prompt them.

Vocabulaire

Le croque-monsieur
Toasted sandwich
Le beurre
Butter
Le pain
Bread
Le fromage
Cheese
Les oeufs
Eggs
Le poulet rôti
Roast chicken
Un hamburger
A hamburger

Une baguette
A french stick
Une salade
A salad
Des frites
Chips
Un croissant
A croissant
Une soupe
A soup
Une pizza
A pizza
Une crêpe
A pancake

La crème brulée
Baked custard
La confiture
Jam
Les céréales
Cereal
Les bonbons
Sweets
Le chocolat
Chocolate
J'aime
I like
Je déteste
I hate

Teaching Ideas

Materials: Copy a set of food pictures provided in this chapter pages 57 (colour if time)
Cut out each item and enlarge. A collage can also be made showing all the items

The teacher spreads the flashcards out face up, points to them and names them in turn, the **children repeat**. To reinforce this vocabulary the flashcards are held up and the teacher demonstrates **"J'aime"** and **"Je déteste"** using different food items. The children then take turns in saying their likes and dislikes using the cards.

 Cocorico Books © Zara Mercer & Margaret Mckee 2009

Soixante

Dialogue au café 1

Le Serveur:- Que désirez-vous?

Maman:- Claire, tu veux une **boisson?**

Claire:- Oui maman, je voudrais une **limonade** s'il te plaît.

Maman:- Et toi Luc?

Luc:- Moi, je voudrais **un coca.**

Le Serveur:- Alors, une **limonade** et **un coca,** et vous?

Maman:- Pour moi, **un café** s'il vous plaît.

Papa:- Et pour moi, **un thé**, merci.

Garçon:- Voila **une limonade, un coca** pour madame **un café**. Et pour monsieur **un thé.**

Les quatres:- Merci!

Soixante et un

Dialogue au café 2

Le Serveur :- Bonjour, que désirez-vous?

Maman :- Bonjour, Je voudrais <u>une pizza</u> et <u>une salade</u> s'il vous plaît

Papa :- Moi, Je voudrais <u>une omelette</u> s'il vous plaît. Et toi Charlotte?

Charlotte :- Je voudrais <u>une soupe</u>

Louise :- Moi, je voudrais <u>une pizza</u> aussi.

Le Serveur :- Alors, <u>deux pizzas</u>, <u>une salade</u>, <u>une omelette</u>, et pour la petite, <u>une soupe</u>!

Les quatre :- Merci!

Cocorico Books © Zara Mercer & Margaret Mckee 2009

Soixante-deux

Menu

～ Entrée ～

Paté	3 Euros
Soupe	3 Euros
Salade	4 Euros

～ Plat Principal ～

Steak-Frites	6 Euros
Pizza	5 Euros
Omelette	4 Euros
Spaghettis	4 Euros
Salade Composée	4 Euros

(avec poulet ou thon)

～ Dessert ～

Mousse au chocolat	2 Euros
Tarte aux pommes	3 Euros
Gateau ã la crème	3 Euros
Crème brulée	3 Euros
Salade de fruits	2 Euros

Cocorico Books © Zara Mercer & Margaret Mckee 2009

Mots Mêlés

Au café

O	P	Z	E	Z	S	Y	S	F	E	E	U	C	N	N
X	M	F	E	H	X	S	R	K	H	U	R	H	S	S
T	A	E	A	F	E	G	A	T	E	A	U	O	C	A
C	E	E	L	T	F	J	V	D	D	C	Z	C	C	N
W	N	B	I	E	S	N	E	Z	Z	O	L	O	P	D
E	P	R	C	Y	T	D	N	E	B	C	Q	L	O	W
S	F	D	U	Z	A	T	C	G	A	A	S	A	P	I
L	C	I	S	N	K	E	E	P	V	Q	A	T	X	C
R	Y	B	O	R	Y	Y	Y	K	S	D	C	B	Q	H
X	Y	M	J	R	P	H	P	I	W	D	N	A	R	S
Z	I	I	G	D	T	C	R	O	T	M	Q	M	T	T
L	L	A	U	L	U	J	S	C	U	Z	E	G	W	W
T	D	P	L	K	A	D	Q	P	W	L	B	P	K	K
G	U	D	Q	F	D	C	Q	J	L	S	E	Q	E	E
I	X	S	L	C	Z	Q	E	C	S	I	B	T	Q	Q

(un) café   (une) glace   (un) poulet
(un) chocolat   (un) gâteau   (un) sandwich
(un) coca   (une) limonade
(des) frites   (une) omelette

Cocorico Books © Zara Mercer & Margaret Mckee 2009

Soixante-quatre

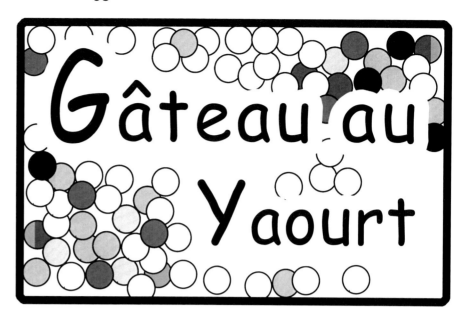

Gâteau au Yaourt

Préparation: environ 15 min

Cuisson : environ 45 min

INGRÉDIENTS (POUR 4 PERSONNES) :
Use the yoghurt pot to measure the other ingrediants

- 1 yaourt nature
  Dont on prend le pot pour mesurer
- 2 pots de farine
- 2 pots de sucre
- 1/2 pot d'huile
- 3 œufs

Préparation

1. Préchauffer le four à 150°C.
2. Verser les ingrédients dans un bol et mélanger pour obtenir une pâte liquide.
3. Huiler et fariner un moule à gâteau
4. Verser cette pâte dans le moule et enfourner. Cuire pendant 45 minutes.
5. **Bon appétit!**

Cuire: *To cook*	**Huile** : *Oil*
Farine : *Flour*	**Moule** : *Tin*
Préchauffer : *Preheat*	**Pot** : *Pot*
Sucre : *Sugar*	**Oeuf** : *Egg*

EN FRANCE
Leçon 1
"La culture"

Vocabulaire

L'école — The school
Le goûter — Snack time
Le déjeuner — Lunch
La sieste — A nap

L'uniforme — The uniform
Les vacances — The holidays
Le stage — Training
Le repas — The meal

GREETINGS AND REVISION

Revise **au café**.
Play a quick role play or use food flashcards page 57-58 and play a game of **"J'aime / Je déteste"** page 60.

Teaching Ideas

Materials: Copies of the "La Culture Française" fact sheet page 67

Give out copies of **"La culture" fact sheet** and read it aloud (if the children are too young). **Go through the content** with the children, asking them to **relate** their **holiday experiences** and **knowledge** of **France** with the lesson material.

Compare each segment of **"La Culture Française"** with the children's own culture and make a parallel with their lives in England, discussing the similarities and differences.

Cocorico Books © Zara Mercer & Margaret Mckee 2009   **Soixante-six**

Culture française

Les colonies de vacances
In France children go to the "colonies de vacances" (holiday camps) all around France they are looked after by paid "animateurs" (teenagers 16 to 21). These animateurs undergo a 2 week training course (stage). ⑨

La Fête Nationale
The national day of France is on the 14th of July.
It is a public holiday with street processions taking place through out the day ending with firework displays all over France ⑪

Le Goûter
French Children have a meal at home called a Goûter at 4:30pm. This is usually the time they celebrate their birthdays with their friends from school. ④

La Santé
French children rarely take snacks to school ①

À Midi
Lunch hour in France is 2 hours long and most children go home to eat. Lunch in France is a bigger meal than the evening meal. ⑥

Mercredi
Primary school children don't go to school on Wednesdays. ③

Laïcité
Children in France do not have any religious lessons, instead, they learn to cook, to run a home and to be a good French citizen.
This subject is called "Education Civique". ⑩

Le Dîner
Most children eat evening meals later than in England with their parents. ⑧

L'uniforme
In France children don't usually wear a uniform. ②

La Sièste
In the infant school, small beds are provided in a quiet room for children to take a nap (sièste) after lunch. ⑦

L'école
French children start school early; 8:30am. They finish at 4pm or 4:30pm ⑤

Cocorico Books © Zara Mercer & Margaret Mckee 2009

Soixante-sept

En France
Leçon 2
"La fête de fin d'année!"

Vocabulaire

La Marseillaise — The French national anthem
Pain au chocolat — Chocolate bun
Un verre — A glass
Bon appétit — Enjoy your meal
Bonnes vacances — Happy holidays
Une serviette — A napkin
La grenadine — Pomegranate juice
Une paille — A straw
Un drapeau — A flag
Les jeux — Games
Danser — To dance
Serveur/euse — Waiter/waitress

Party Preparation

- Decorate the room with pictures of France and French and English flags from page 69. These should be coloured by the children.
- Cover a few tables with checked fabric.
- Buy some croissants, pains au chocolat and enough grenadine (pomegranate juice) for everyone.
- Provide some French music for dancing or just ambiance.
- Ask the children to dress up for the occasion in berets, stripy t-shirts, nautical outfits.

Party Ideas

Materials: Tea towels / notebook / etc. to use as waiter props

Choose a **few children** to be **waiters** (to help out with serving). The remaining children sit at tables and **ask for their refreshments in French (Je voudrais...)** Use the music to dance to or play a game (ask the children to choose a favourite game played during the term.)

Most importantly - **Have fun!**

 Cocorico Books © Zara Mercer & Margaret Mckee 2009

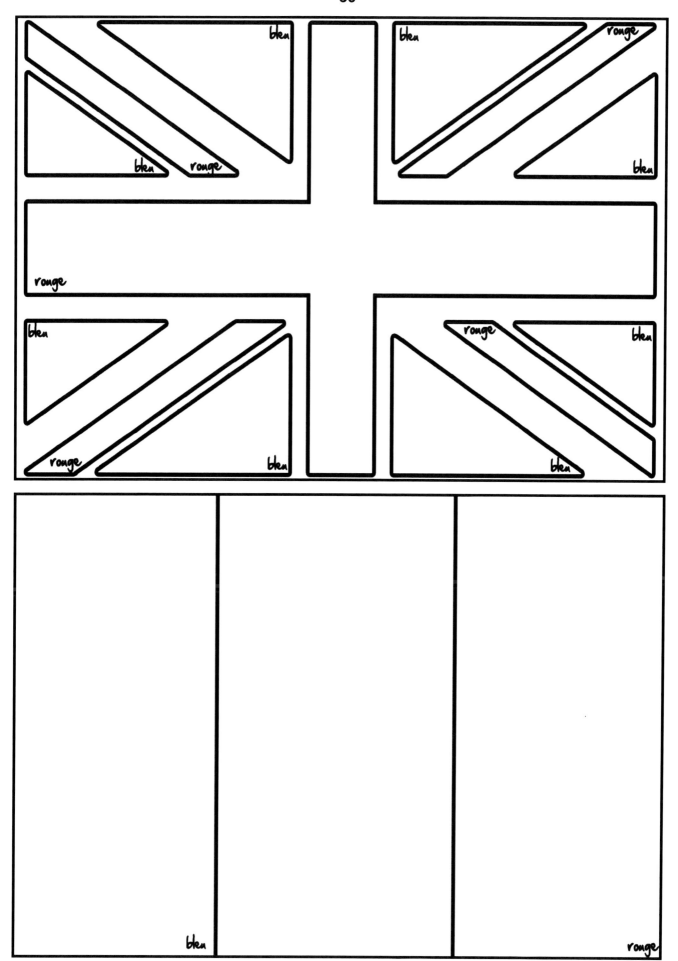

LES FÊTES
Leçon 1
"Les Jours de Vacances"

Vocabulaire

Les Vacances — The holidays
La fête des rois — Twelfth night
Le roi — The king
La reine — The queen
Une gallette — A cake
Un bouchon — A traffic "jam"
Une cloche — A bell
Le soleil — The sun
La mer — The sea
La forêt — The forest

Teaching Ideas

Start a discussion with the class by comparing British holidays with French ones, see the calendar below:

Le 6 février - La Fête des Rois

French children share a cake called **"La galette des rois"** in which a small china figurine (Christmas character) called **"La fève"** is hidden. The lucky child who discovers it in his / her portion becomes the king or queen for the rest of the day. It is traditional that as slices of the cake are being served, the youngest person hides under the table and decides who is going to get the next piece by touching their leg.

Février - Mardi gras

Mardi Gras literally means **"Fat Tuesday"**. It is the carnival period which ends on the day before Ash Wednesday. Children wear disguises and in the evening they parade through the streets. They also make pancakes which they learn to flip in the air.

 Cocorico Books © Zara Mercer & Margaret Mckee 2009

"Les Jours de Vacances"

Activités

Mars/Avril - Pâques
At Easter it is traditional to hunt for eggs hidden in the garden. All the church bells are rung at the same time on Easter Sunday and chocolate bells are bought and eaten.

Juin - Fête de la Musique
Many concerts of all types of music such as jazz, classical and pop are held throughout France for 2 weeks. Schools hold open days dedicated to music.

Juillet/Août - Les Vacances
Schools in France close early in July. Many children go to **summer camps (colonies de vacances)** to meet children of their own age, to explore different parts of the country and to enjoy adventure activities.

Août - L'embouteillage
In August, most businesses and shops close for the holidays. Everyone takes to the road in their cars and creates **mega traffic jams! (Bouchons)**.

Soixante et onze

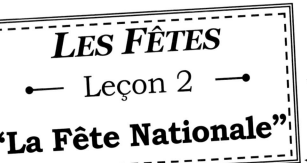

LES FÊTES
— Leçon 2 —
"La Fête Nationale"

CELEBRATE
« LE QUATORZE JUILLET »

Prepare a party for the children celebrating **Bastille Day** - the French national holiday. Celebrate it as close to the 14th of July as possible.

Vocabulaire

Vive la France!
Long live France!

Vive l'Angleterre!
Long live England!

Salle à manger
Dining room

Pains au chocolat
Chocolate pastry

Le quatorze juillet
The 14th of July

Une grenadine
Pomegranate syrup

Teaching Ideas

Materials:	French & English flags photocopied and coloured from page 69
	Checked tablecloths
	Croissants & pains au chocolat
	Drinks (pomegranate juice, orange juice, etc)
	Plastic cups
	French Quiz page 73

Transform the classroom into a "**salle à manger**". Decorate the room with **French** and **English flags** coloured in by the children. Cover a few tables with **tablecloths** and put out the **croissants**, **pains au chocolat** and drinks.

Encourage the children to ask for the food and drink in French eg:

"Je voudrais un croissant s'il vous plaît"
"Je voudrais un jus d'orange s'il vous plaît"

Some children can help with serving. The activity can be more fun if the **children dress up in French clothes** for instance a **beret** or a **striped t-shirt** and a **moustache**. Divide the class into teams, one team per table and have a competition using the French quiz on page 73 with **prizes**.

 Cocorico Books © Zara Mercer & Margaret Mckee 2009

Soixante-douze

Quiz: La France

1. What is the capital of France?
2. What is the name of the Sea south of France?
3. What is the name of the sea between France and England?
4. Name three cities in France.
5. How many countries share a border with France?
6. Name these countries.
7. When is the "Fête de la bastille"?
8. What is the name of the French Flag?
9. What is the name of the theme park north of Paris?
10. Name 2 special French products.
11. How do you say "Thank you" in French?
12. How do you say "Please" in French?
13. In which French city do you find the river Seine?
14. What is the name of the little soft hat worn by French men?
15. What moon-shaped item do French people eat for breakfast?
16. What is the name of the Paris underground?
17. What is the currency used in France?

Answers

1. Paris   2. La Mer Méditerranée   3. La Manche   4. Marseille, Lyon, Cherbourg etc.   5. Six   6. Belgique, Allemagne, Suisse, Italie, Luxembourg, L'Espagne   7. 14 Juillet   8. Le Tricolore   9. Eurodisney   10. Wine, Cheese, Perfume, etc   11. Merci   12. S'il vous plait   13. Paris   14. Beret   15. Croissant   16. Le Métro   17. L'Euro

 Cocorico Books © Zara Mercer & Margaret Mckee 2009

la Tour Eiffel

Dessinez la partie droite de La Tour Eiffel

LES FÊTES
Leçon 3
"Noël"

Vocabulaire

Le Père Noël *Father Christmas*	**Des jouets** *Toys*
Joyeux Noël! *Happy Christmas!*	**Une église** *A church*
Un sapin *A Christmas tree*	**Des cadeaux** *Presents*
Des boules *Baubles*	**Un sac** *A bag*
Des bougies *Candles*	**Un vélo** *A bicycle*
Des guirlandes *Tinsel*	**Une poupée** *A doll*
Une lettre *A letter*	**Une dinde** *A turkey*
Une bûche de Noël *A Christmas Yule Log*	**Traîneau** *A sleigh*

GREETINGS, REVISION ROLEPLAY

Start the lesson by decorating the classroom with Christmas cards and banners using the words from the *vocabulaire* list.

Teaching Ideas

Materials: Copy and cut out 2 sets of the Christmas images on page 78

Write **"Joyeux Noël"** on the board or on a large piece of card, read and repeat it with the children.

Discuss with the class how they celebrate Christmas in their own homes. Compare this with the way in which **Noël is celebrated in France**. Refer to "Noël en France" page 76.

Use the Christmas images to play "Pairs" page 5.
Make the Christmas card from page 82.

Cocorico Books © Zara Mercer & Margaret Mckee 2009

"Noël"

"Noël en France"

- The main Christmas celebration in France is on Christmas Eve. Families have a very special meal on this evening. They usually have different types of seafood and lots of little dishes filled with all sorts of sweet and savoury food. The table looks like a grand banquet.

- For dessert, a Christmas Yule Log (Une Bûche) made with cream and chocolate is served. It is a tradition to have 12 puddings with the meal, one for each of the disciples. Children stay up late after the family dinner, as they sometimes go to midnight mass.

- French children clean their shoes until they shine and then they place them by the fire-place hoping that Father Christmas ("Papa Noël") will fill them with presents.

- Christmas story-telling is also an old tradition. These stories are usually about people who are less fortunate than themselves. This makes the children appreciate their own warm home and family surroundings.

- The following day, Christmas Day, the French eat roast turkey, goose or chicken accompanied by special vegetables and delicious gravy.

"Noël"

Le 23 décembre .... se prépare pour Noël. Les enfants décorent .... avec .... et .... Au sommet du sapin il y a .... ou .... Maman allume ...., elle les place sur .... Les enfants nettoient bien leurs chaussures parce-que .... va mettre .... dedans. Il fait le tour du monde dans son .... pour donner ....à tous les enfants sages. .... se met à table pour un grand repas de Noël. Ils mangent de ....et beaucoup de belles choses, comme dessert il y a ...., un délicieux gâteau au chocolat.

  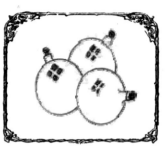 

La Famille — Le Sapin — Des Boules — Un Ange

Une Étoile — Des Guirlandes — Des Bougies

Père Noël — Des Cadeaux — La Cheminée

La Bûche de Noël — Traîneau — La Dinde

Cher Père Noël

Je m'appelle _____ j'ai _____ ans.

J'habite à _____ avec _____

Pour Noël, je voudrais:

Je travaille bien à l'école, J'aide ma mère à la maison. Je suis gentil avec mes amis.

Merci Père Noël de considérer ma liste.

Tous mes souhaits de bonne chance avec le long voyage que tu vas bientôt faire pour distribuer tous les cadeaux aux enfants du monde.

Mots Mêlés

Noël

E	F	P	A	E	G	D	C	A	D	E	A	U	P	V
I	K	X	H	N	F	U	U	J	E	K	K	C	E	D
T	P	C	C	C	F	D	I	U	B	P	U	Q	R	S
G	U	O	D	G	L	K	U	R	S	O	W	Z	E	D
B	J	E	G	L	I	S	E	Q	L	F	U	O	N	B
D	E	R	X	K	R	N	N	J	H	A	P	L	O	H
S	S	D	I	N	D	E	Z	O	M	V	N	U	E	F
P	A	E	C	H	A	U	S	S	U	R	E	D	L	I
T	G	P	C	C	K	B	O	U	G	I	E	S	E	W
K	M	J	I	D	E	T	P	E	Z	X	J	B	T	T
E	N	F	X	N	E	Z	W	Y	U	H	M	Y	N	E

(une) bougie   (une) chaussure   (un) sapin
(une) boule   (une) dinde   (une) église
(une) bûche   (une) guirlande
(un) cadeau   Père Noël

Mots Mêlés

Les Fêtes

S	X	J	V	T	T	V	J	J	P	B	C	W	N	I
A	F	I	E	F	N	G	P	R	J	U	Q	P	J	F
N	O	Ë	L	W	D	G	A	T	E	A	U	M	O	Q
W	T	J	T	A	F	A	Q	C	T	O	J	U	E	S
X	F	T	K	E	Q	G	U	Y	P	O	B	X	Q	V
U	V	E	A	B	S	K	E	G	L	I	S	E	P	A
V	A	C	A	N	C	E	S	V	I	F	L	U	V	G
X	J	A	H	C	W	B	V	M	E	E	Q	A	F	B
V	E	R	G	A	C	K	S	S	C	A	D	E	A	U
K	E	T	Q	H	N	O	I	K	M	O	Z	T	Y	M
K	O	Ë	L	S	P	S	S	U	F	X	E	D	X	P
Q	Z	F	D	O	G	F	O	T	H	Q	I	K	H	Y
M	K	T	R	U	B	A	N	N	U	Z	Y	I	B	K
T	I	U	M	O	Q	F	D	F	A	M	I	L	L	E
A	H	V	A	W	V	C	W	F	X	Z	E	U	V	Q

Noël   (la) Carte   (le) Cadeau
(la) fête   (la) Chanson   (le) ruban
(les) vacances (l') église   (la) famille
Pâques   (le) Costume   (le) gâteau

 Cocorico Books © Zara Mercer & Margaret Mckee 2009

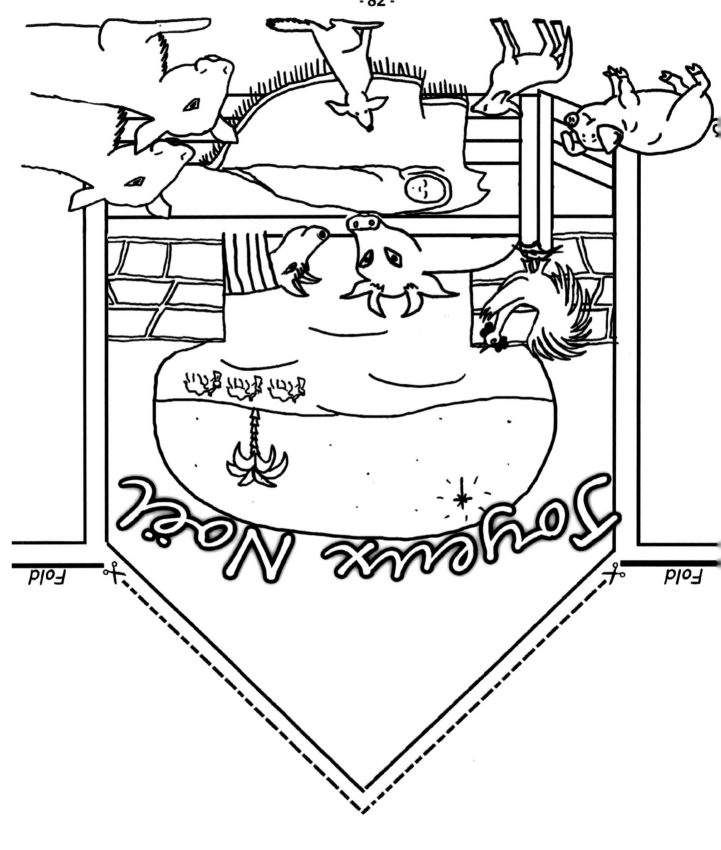

La Carte de Pâques -83-

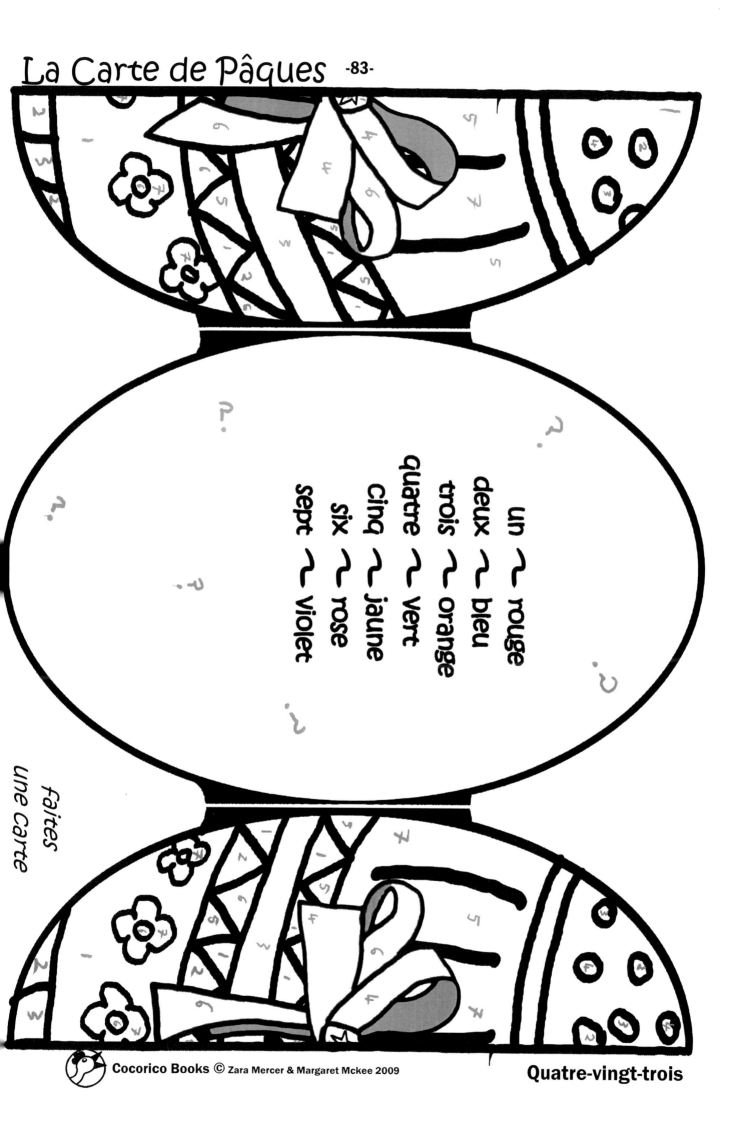

un ~ rouge
deux ~ bleu
trois ~ orange
quatre ~ vert
cinq ~ jaune
six ~ rose
sept ~ violet

faites une carte

Cocorico Books © Zara Mercer & Margaret Mckee 2009

Quatre-vingt-trois

Chantons ensemble!

"Bonjour ça va?"

A Variation of "If you're happy and you know it..." Use the following actions to the tune

CHORUS
Bonjour les enfants comment ça va?
Bonjour les enfants comment ça va?
Ça va bien, ça va mal, ça va bien, comme ci comme ça,
Bonjour les enfants comment ça va?

"ça va bien"

"ça va mal"

CHORUS
Bonjour les enfants quel âge as-tu?
Bonjour les enfants quel âge as-tu?
J'ai un, deux, trois quatre, cinq, sept, six, sept,
Bonjour les enfants quel âge as-tu?

CHORUS
Bonjour les enfants où habites-tu?
Bonjour les enfants où habites-tu?
J'habite avec mon père, ma mère, ma soeur, mon frère
Bonjour les enfants où habites-tu?

"comme ci comme ça"

"Quel âge as-tu?"

Hold up the correct number of fingers as you sing each age

CHORUS
Quel âge as-tu, quel âge as-tu, un, deux, trois?
Quel âge as-tu, quel âge as-tu, quatre, cinq, six?
Quel âge as-tu, quel âge as-tu, sept-huit, neuf, dix?

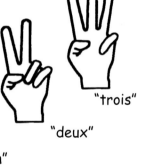
"trois"
"deux"
"un"

Cocorico Books © Zara Mercer & Margaret Mckee 2009

Chantons ensemble!

"Savez-vous planter les choux?"

Savez-vous planter les choux,
À la mode, à la mode,
Savez-vous planter les choux
À la mode de chez nous?

On les plante avec le pied
À la mode, à la mode,
On les plante avec le pied,
À la mode de chez nous.

"Joyeux Anniversaire"

To the tune of "Happy Birthday to you"

Joyeux anniversaire, joyeux anniversaire,
Joyeux anniversaire, **(name)** joyeux anniversaire!

Quel âge as-tu, quel âge as-tu,
quel âge as-tu (**name**) quel âge as-tu?

"Orange, Rouge, Bleu"

To the tune of "3 Blind Mice"

Orange, rouge, bleu,
Orange, rouge, bleu,
Jaune, vert, marron
Jaune, vert, marron
Et voici les couleurs,
Et voici les couleurs,
Et voici les couleurs, noir et blanc

 Cocorico Books © Zara Mercer & Margaret Mckee 2009

Quatre-vingt-cinq

"Sur le pont d'Avignon"

CHORUS
Sur le pont d'Avignon,
L'on y danse l'on y danse,
Sur le pont d'Avignon
On y danse tous en rond.

VERSE
Les professeurs font comm' ça
Et puis encor' comm' ça.

CHORUS

VERSE
Les écoliers font comm' ca
Et puis encore comm' ca

CHORUS

VERSE
Les demoiselles font comm' ca
Et puis encor' comm' ca.

"Alouette, gentille alouette"

Each verse starts with the preceding one and adds an extra word on to the end "et la ...."

REFRAIN
Alouette, gentill' alouette,
Alouette, je te plumerais.

VERSE 1
Je te plumerais la tête (x2)
Et la tête (x2)
Alouhette x2
Ohhh!

VERSE 2
Je te plumerais, la tête (x2)
Et la tête (x2)
Et le bec (x2)
Et la ... etc (x2)
Alouhette x2
Ohhh!

Je te plumerais, le cou ... le ventre ... le dos ... les ailes ... la queue ... les

 Cocorico Books © Zara Mercer & Margaret Mckee 2009